PIANO / VOCAL / GUITAR

budgetbooks

COUNTRY SONGS

ISBN 0-634-04070-7

Visit Hal Leonard Online at
www.halleonard.com

CONTENTS

ABILENE

Words and Music by LESTER BROWN, JOHN D. LOUDERMILK and BOB GIBSON

G
B7
C
I sit a - lone most ev - 'ry night, watch those trains
G
A7
D7
pull out of sight. Don't I wish they were car - ry - ing me back to
G
C
G
B7
Ab - i - lene, my Ab - i - lene. Ab - i - lene, Ab - i - lene,
C
G
A7
pret - ti - est town I've ev - er seen. Wom - en there don't

D7 G C G Am7 D7

treat you mean __ in Ab - i - lene, my Ab - i - lene.

G B7 C

Crowd - ed cit - y, there ain't noth - ing free; noth - ing in this

G A7 D7

town for me. Wish to the Lord that I could be __ in Ab - i -

1 G C G

lene, sweet __ Ab - i - lene.

2 G C G

lene, sweet __ Ab - i - lene.

ALWAYS ON MY MIND

Words and Music by WAYNE THOMPSON, MARK JAMES and JOHNNY CHRISTOPHER

F/A
B♭
F/A
Gm
3fr
B♭/F
B♭/D
said and done,
sec - ond best,
I just nev - er took the time.
girl, I'm sor - ry I was blind.
C7
Dm7
C7/E
F
To Coda
B♭
C7
You were al - ways on my mind.
You were al - ways on my
1
F
B♭
C7
2
F
B♭
C7
F
C/E
Dm
F/C
mind.
mind.
Tell me,
B♭
F/A
Gm
3fr
C7
F
C/E
tell me that your sweet love has-n't died.
Give

Dm
F/C
B♭
F/A
Gm
3fr
C
me, give me one more chance to keep you sat - is - fied, sat - is -
F
D.S. al Coda
fied.
CODA
B♭
You are al-ways on my
C7
F
C/E
Dm
F/C
mind.
B♭
Am
Gm7
3fr
C7
F
You are al - ways on my mind.
rit.

AIN'T GOIN' DOWN
('Til the Sun Comes Up)

Words and Music by KIM WILLIAMS,
GARTH BROOKS and KENT BLAZY

C
rub - ber squeal - ing, gears a jam - ming, lo - cal Coun - try sta - tion just a
but she's gon - na keep him wait - ing. First, a bite to eat and then they're
G
blar - ing on the ra - di - o. Pick him up at sev - en and they're
head - ing to the hon - ky - tonk, but loud crowds and line danc - ing
D
head - ing to the ro - de - o. Ma - ma's on the front porch,
just ain't what they real - ly want. Drive out to the boon - docks
G
scream - ing out a warn - ing: "Girl, you'd bet - ter get your red head
and park down by the creek, where it's George Strait 'til real late and

1
back in bed be - fore the morn-ing."
danc - ing cheek to cheek.
2
C
They ain't go - ing down 'til the sun comes _ up, ain't _
G
Bb
— giv - ing in 'til they get e-nough.
Go - ing 'round the world in a

pick - up
truck.
G
no chord
To Coda
F
G
Ain't go - ing down 'til the sun comes up.
F
G
Ten 'til twelve is wine and danc - ing. Mid - night starts the hard ro - manc - ing.
Six o' - clock on Sat - ur - day, her folks don't know he's on his way. The

C
G
One o' - clock that truck is rock - ing. Two is com - ing, still no stop - ping.
stalls are clean, the hors - es fed. They say she's ground - ed 'til she's dead. Well,
D
Break to check the clock at three. They're right at where they wan - ta be and
here he comes a - round the bend, slow - ing down. She's jump - ing in.
G
four o' - clock get up and go - ing. Five o' - clock that roost - er's crow - ing.
Hey, Mom, your daugh - ter's gone and there they go a - gain. Hey.
Hey.
Instrumental solo each time

C
G
D
1 G
2 G
Solo ends
Yeah, they
D.S. al Coda
Solo ends
They
CODA
G
D.S.S. and Fade
sun comes up.
Yeah.

ALIBIS

Words and Music by
RANDY BOUDREAUX

Moderate Country waltz (♫ played as ♩ ♪ triplet)

E C#m E

mf R.H.

C#m E C#m

She knows ev - 'ry move that a man
once thought that love was - n't just

A B E

could make. She knows ev - 'ry trick
a game; her feel - in's once came

C#m A

in the book. She
from the heart.

E C#m E
knows how to give. She knows how to
One day I gave her a wed - din'
C#m F#m A
take. 'Cause so man - y times she's been
ring. And one night I tore all those
B7 E
tak - en and fooled by those
feel - in's a - part with my
al - i - bis and
C#m E E7
ly - in' eyes and all the best lines. Lord knows she's

A
E/G#
F#m
B
heard 'em all.
She's been
E
C#m
E
cheat - ed on and pushed a - round and left a - lone. Lord
E7
A
E/G#
knows what I've put her through. And
F#m
B
F#m
boy you can bet if a move can be made,

B
A
To Coda
B
1
she knows how to make one on
E
C#m
E
C#m
you.
She
2
B
D.S. al Coda
her own
CODA
B
E
one on you.
C#m
E
C#m
E

ALL MY EX'S LIVE IN TEXAS

Words and Music by LYNDIA J. SHAFER
and SANGER D. SHAFER

Fdim7
A
love to be.
But all my ex - 's live in
E7
To Coda
Tex - as.
(1-2) And that's why I hang my hat in Ten - nes -
(D.S.) There -
A
G#
A
see.
Ro - san - na's down in
I re - mem - ber that old
dim.
Bm
Tex - ar - ka - na; want - ed me to push her broom. And
Fri - o Riv - er where I learned to swim. And it

E7
sweet I - lene's in Ab - i - lene; she for - got I hung the
brings to mind an - oth - er time where I wore my wel - come
A
moon. And Al - li - son in Gal - ves - ton
thin. By tran - scen - den - tal med - i - ta - tion
Bm
some - how lost her san - i - ty.
I go there each night.
B7
And Dim - ples who now
But I al - ways come back
lives in Tem - ple's got the law
to my - self
E7
look - in' for me.
long be - fore day - light.
1
2
D.S. al Coda
cresc.

CODA
E
A
fore I re - side in Ten - nes - see.
D
D♯
E
D
D♯
Some folks think I'm hid - ing.
E
D
D♯
E
It's been ru - mored that I died.
But I'm a - live and well
A
D6
D♯dim7
A/E
A6/9
in Ten - nes - see.

AMAZED

Words and Music by MARV GREEN,
CHRIS LINDSEY and AIMEE MAYO

*Recorded a half step lower.

A
E
Ba - by, when you touch me, I can feel how much you love me,
Your hair all a - round me; ba - by, you sur - round me.
F♯m
D
and it just blows me a - way.
You touch ev - 'ry place in my heart.
C
G
I've nev - er been this close to an - y - one or an - y - thing.
Oh, it feels like the first time ev - 'ry time.
Am
Am7
F
I can hear your thoughts. I can see your dreams.
I wan - na spend the whole night in your eyes.

D
A
I don't know how you do what you do.
I'm so in love with you.
It just keeps get-tin' bet - ter.
Bm
G
I wan-na spend the rest of my life
with you by my side
for-ev-er and ev-
er.
F
Ev-'ry lit-tle thing that you do,

1.
G
A
baby, I'm amazed by you.
2.
G
A
C
D
baby, I'm amazed by you.
A
C
G
Dsus4
D
G
Ev-'ry lit-tle thing that you do.
A
Bm
G
I'm so in love with you.
It just keeps get-tin' bet - ter.

D
A
I wan-na spend the rest of my life with you by my side
Bm
G
F
for-ev-er and ev - er.
Ev-'ry lit-tle thing that you do,
G
F/A
oh,
ev-'ry lit-tle thing that you do,
Freely
G/B
G
Tempo I
A
Tacet
ba-by, I'm a-mazed by you.
mp
rit.

ANY OLD TIME

Words and Music by
JIMMIE RODGERS

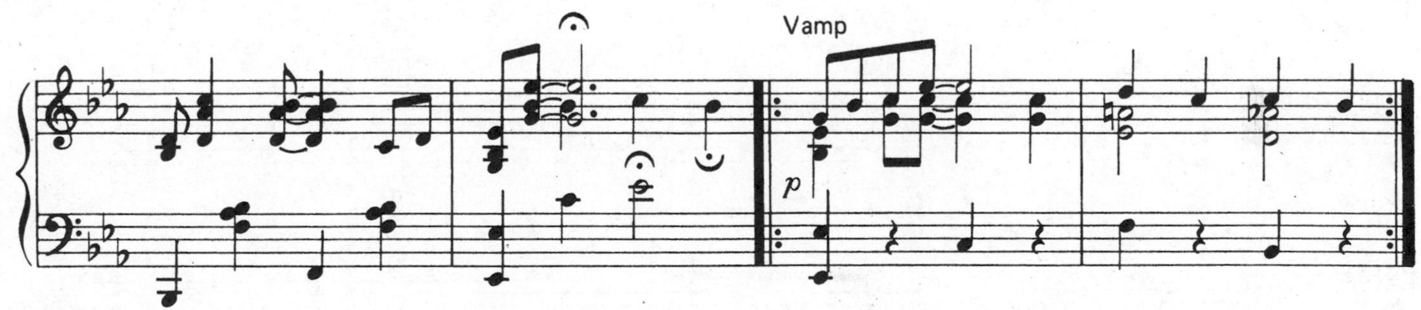

Eb
say, at first I thought I would tell you to
F7
Bb7
Eb
tra - vel on the oth - er way, but in my mem - o - ry
Eb7
Ab
lin - gers, all you once were__ to me
F7
C7
Bb7
I'm going to give you an - oth - er chance_ to prove what you can

Eb
Bb7
Eb
Eb7
be.
An - y old time
you want to
p - f
come back home,
Ab7
drop me a line
and say no more you'll roam,
Eb
Bb7
you had your chance to play the game

Eb
F7
fair, when you left me sweet - heart, you
Bb7
Eb
Bb7
Eb
on - ly left a load of care.
Now that you're
Ab
Eb
down I'm go - ing to stick by you, if
F7
Bb7
you will on - ly say your roam - ing days are

Eb
through,
You'll find me here like the
Eb7
Ab
Bb7
day you left me a - lone,
An - y old time
you want to come back home.
1 Eb
F7
Bb7
Eb
2 Eb
Ab7
Eb
home.

ANYMORE

Words and Music by TRAVIS TRITT
and JILL COLUCCI

G F

out of my eyes any-more.
-dle an-y-where next to you. Mm hm.

G F

My tears no lon-ger wait-
My heart can't take the beat-

G F G

-ing. My re-sis-tance ain't that strong.
-ing not hav-ing you to hold.

F G E

My mind keeps re-cre-at-ing a love with you a-lone.
A small voice keeps re-peat-ing deep in-side my soul.

Am
F
G
And I'm tired of pre - tend - ing
It says I can't keep pre - tend - ing
F
G
1 C
F
I don't love you an - y - more.
I don't love you an - y - more.
Let me make
2 C
Am
F
I've got to take the chance or let it pass by
Am
G
if I ex - pect to get on with my life.
3
3
3

C
G
F
G
C
G
F
G
F
My tears no long-er wait-
G
F
- ing.
Oh, my re-sis-tance ain't that strong.

G
F
Oh, my mind keeps re - cre - at -
G
E/G#
Am
F
G
- ing a love with you a - lone.
And I'm tired of pre - tend - ing
F
G
C
F
I don't love you an - y - more.
An - y - more.
C
F
C
An - y - more.
rit.

AUCTIONEER

Words and Music by LEROY VAN DYKE
and BUDDY BLACK

(Spoken:) Hey, well all right, Sir, here we go there, and what're ya gonna give for 'em. I'm bid twenty-five, will ya gimme thirty, make it thirty, bid it to buy 'em at thirty dollars on 'er, will ya gimme thirty, now five, who woulda bid it at five, make it five, five bid and now forty dollars on 'er to buy 'em there...

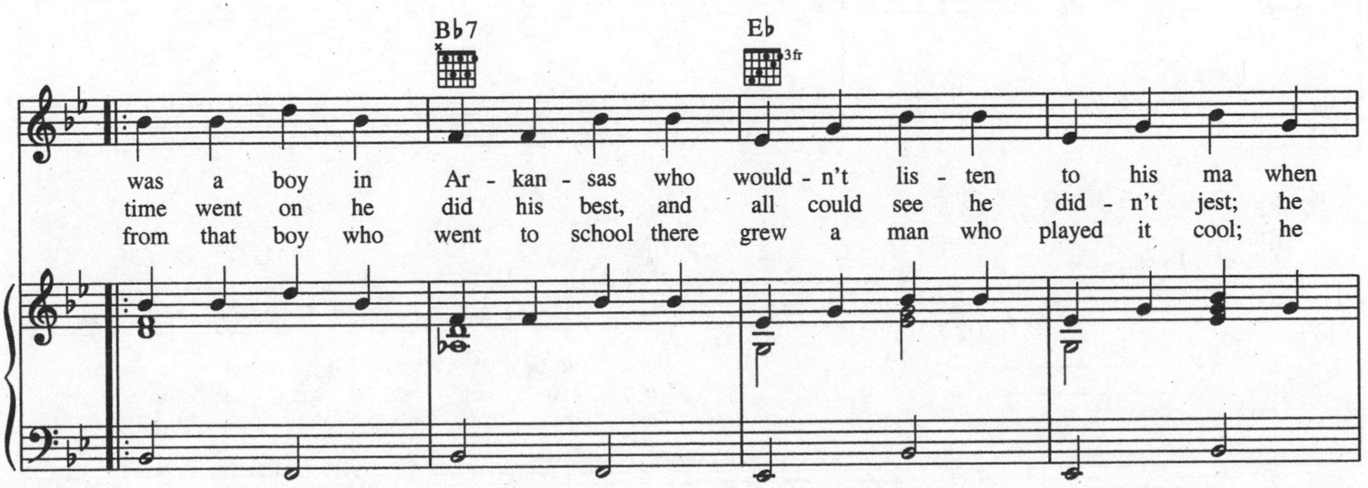

F7
B♭
she told him that he should go to school. He'd
prac - ticed call - ing bids both night and day. His
came back home a full - fledged auc - tion - eer.
B♭7
E♭
3fr
sneak a - way in the af - ter - noon, take a lit - tle walk and
pop would find him be - hind the barn just work - ing up an
Then the peo - ple came from miles a - round just to hear him make that
F7
pret - ty soon you'd find him at the lo - cal auc - tion
aw - ful storm as he tried to im - i - tate the auc - tion -
rhyth - mic sound that filled their hearts with such a hap - py
B♭
E♭
3fr
barn. He'd stand and he'd lis - ten care - ful - ly, then
eer. Then his pop said, "Son, we just can't
cheer. Then his fame spread out from shore to

B♭
C7
pret - ty soon he be - gan to see how the auc - tion - eer could
stand to have a me - di - o - cre man sell - in' things at auc - tion
shore; he had all he could do and more. Had to buy a
F7
B♭
talk so rap - id - ly.
He said, "Oh my, it's
us - ing our good name.
I'll send you off to
plane to get a - round.
Now he's the tops in
B♭7
E♭
3fr
do or die; I've got to learn that auc - tion cry. Got - ta
auc - tion school; then you'll be no - bod - y's fool.
all the land. Let's pause to give that man a hand;
F7
B♭
make my mark and be an auc - tion - eer."
Twen - ty -
You can take your place a - mong the best."
Thir - ty -
he's the best hill - bil - y auc - tion - eer.
For - ty -

B♭7
five dol - lar bid an' now thir - ty dol - lar, thir - ty, will you
five dol - lar bid an' now for - ty dol - lar, for - ty, will you
five dol - lar bid an' now fif - ty dol - lar, fif - ty, will you
E♭7
3
gim - me thir - ty, make it thir - ty, bi - di - di - bom a thir - ty dol - lar,
gim - me for - ty, make it for - ty, bi - di - di - bom a for - ty dol - lar,
gim - me fif - ty, make it fif - ty, bi - di - di - bom a fif - ty dol - lar,
F7
3
3
will you gim - me thir - ty, who - da - da bi - di - da thir - ty dol - lar
will you gim - me for - ty, who - da - da bi - di - da for - ty dol - lar
will you gim - me fif - ty, who - da - da bi - di - da fif - ty dol - lar
B♭
bid.
bid.
bid.
Thir - ty dol - lar bid an' now
For - ty dol - lar bid an' now
Fif - ty dol - lar bid an' now

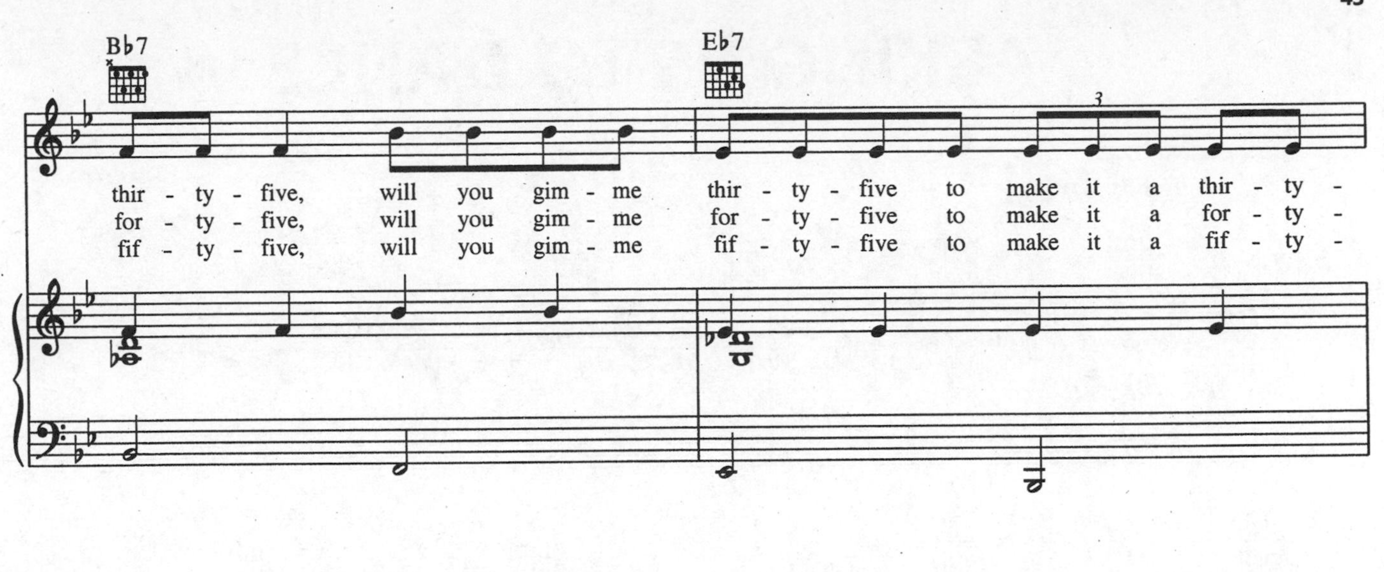

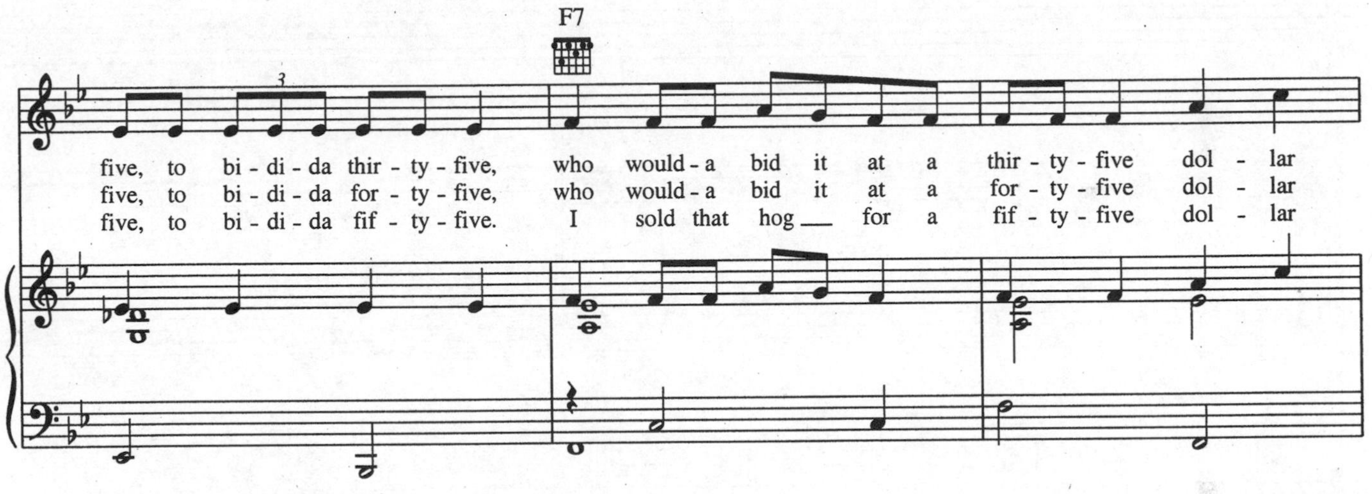

(Spoken:) Hey, well all right, Sir, open the gate an' let 'em out and walk 'em, boys! Here we come with lot number 29 in, what'd ya gonna give for 'em? I'm bid twenty-five, will ya gimme thirty, make it thirty, bid it to buy 'em at thirty dollars on 'er, will you gimme thirty dollars on 'er, now five, thirty-five, an' now the forty dollars on 'er, will you gimme forty, make it forty, now five, forty-five an' now the fifty dollars on 'er, will you gimme fifty, now five, fifty-five, an' now the sixty dollars on 'er, will you gimme sixty, make it sixty, now five, who'd-a bid it at sixty dollars on 'er to buy 'em there...

ASKING US TO DANCE

Words and Music by
HUGH PRESTWOOD

C F

sil - ver hang - ing from the cy - press trees.

Gsus G C Csus

There's a riv - er made of moon - light

C F

flow - ing clear a - cross the lake.

Gsus G

And there's a mil - lion stars just wait - ing to fall for an - y wish we

C F/C C G C/E F G
make. Darling, tonight I am remind-
C F
ed how much these two hearts need romance.
Gsus G
You know it isn't all that of-
You know it isn't very of-
Gsus G C C/E F G
ten you get this kind of chance. Why don't we get caught in this mo-
ten we get this kind of chance. Why don't we get caught in this mo-

C
F
- ment,
- ment,
be vic - tims of ___ sweet cir - cum -
Gsus
G
stance.
To - night I feel ___ like all ___ cre -
Gsus
G
C
Csus
C
Csus
To Coda
a - tion is ask - ing us ___ to dance. ___
C
Csus
C
Csus
There'll be time e - nough ___ to - mor - row

C
Csus
C
Csus
to get back to ___ our dail - y bread. ___
C
Csus
C
But there's some - thing 'bout this eve - ning
F
Gsus
G
that's put this no - tion in ___ my head ___ that heav - en and ___ the earth _ are meet-
C
Csus
C
- ing ___
to - night up - on ___ this ver - y

F
spot.
And all the things _ on earth _ worth hav -
Gsus
G
D.S. al Coda
- ing are things that we've_ al-read-y got.
CODA
C
F/C
C
G
C/E
F
G
C
F
Gsus
G
Gsus
G
C
C/E
F
Repeat and Fade
G

BIG BAD JOHN

Words and Music by
JIMMY DEAN

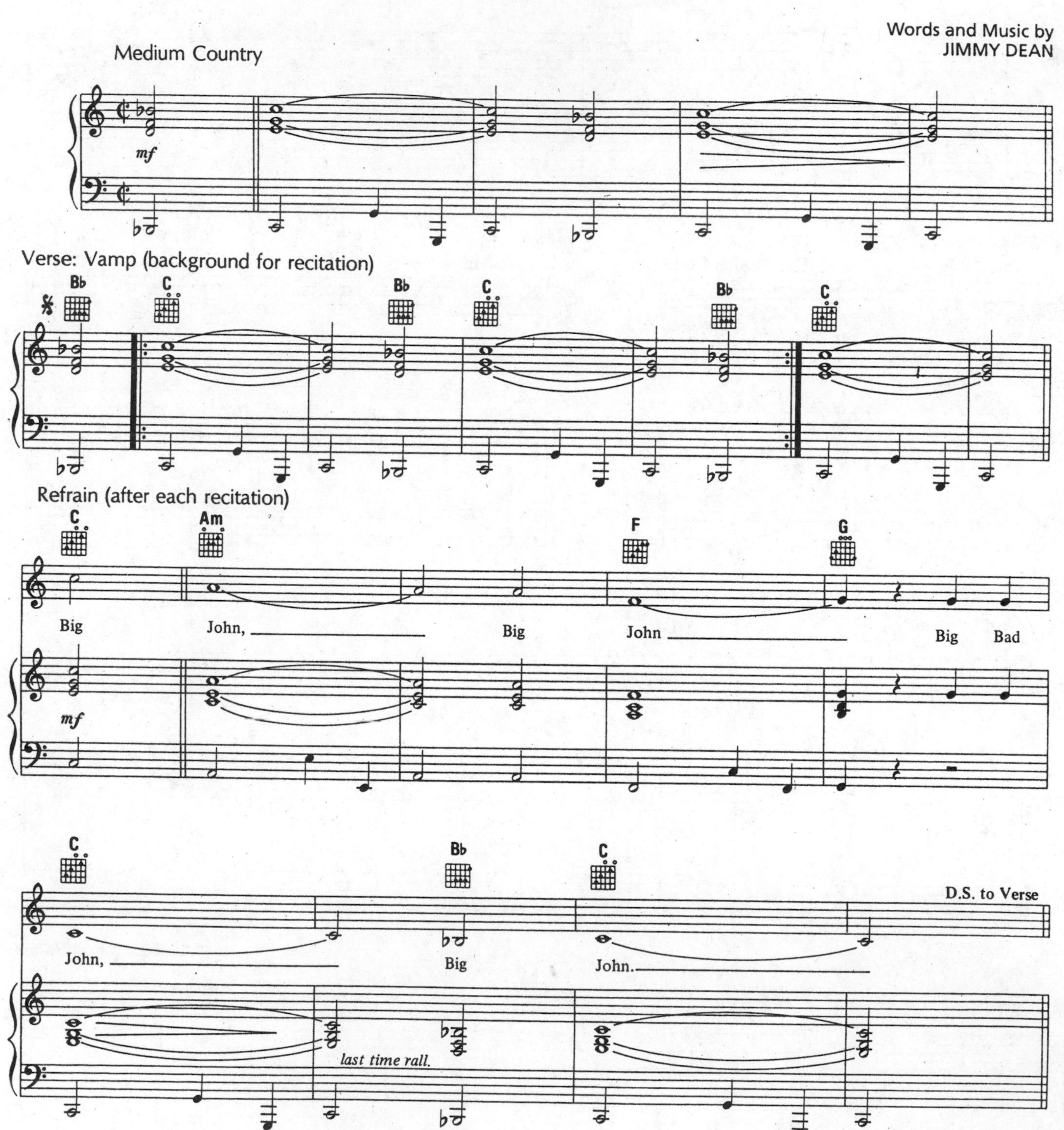

Verse 1. Every morning at the mine you could see him arrive,
He stood six-foot-six and weighed two-forty-five.
Kind of broad at the shoulder and narrow at the hip,
And everybody knew you didn't give no lip to Big John!
(Refrain)

Verse 2. Nobody seemed to know where John called home,
He just drifted into town and stayed all alone.
He didn't say much, a-kinda quiet and shy,
And if you spoke at all, you just said, "Hi" to Big John!
Somebody said he came from New Orleans,
Where he got in a fight over a Cajun queen.
And a crashing blow from a huge right hand
Sent a Louisiana fellow to the promised land. Big John!
(Refrain)

Verse 3. Then came the day at the bottom of the mine
When a timber cracked and the men started crying.
Miners were praying and hearts beat fast,
And everybody thought that they'd breathed their last 'cept John.
Through the dust and the smoke of this man-made hell
Walked a giant of a man that the miners knew well.
Grabbed a sagging timber and gave out with a groan,
And, like a giant oak tree, just stood there alone. Big John!
(Refrain)

Verse 4. And with all of his strength, he gave a mighty shove;
Then a miner yelled out, "There's a light up above!"
And twenty men scrambled from a would-be grave,
And now there's only one left down there to save; Big John!
With jacks and timbers they started back down
Then came that rumble way down in the ground,
And smoke and gas belched out of that mine,
Everybody knew it was the end of the line for Big John!
(Refrain)

Verse 5. Now they never re-opened that worthless pit,
They just placed a marble stand in front of it;
These few words are written on that stand:
"At the bottom of this mine lies a big, big man; Big John!"
(Refrain)

BLUE

Words and Music by
BILL MACK

A
C#7
F#9
3 fr
Blue,
oh, so
Instrumental solo
B7
E7
lone-some for you.
Tears fill my eyes
till I can't
A
D
A
N.C.
C#7
see.
Solo ends
Three o' clock in the morn - ing
Now that it's o - ver,
F#7
here am I
I re - al - ized

B7
E7
To Coda
sit - ting here _ so lone - ly, ___
those _ weak _ words you whis - pered ___
so lone-some I could
were noth-ing but __
D/F#
E7/G#
A
C#7
cry.
Blue, ___
F#9
3 fr
B7
oh, so lone-some for _ you.
Why _ can't _ you be
E7
A
D.S. al Coda
E7
D7/F#
E7/G#
blue ___ o - ver me?

CODA
F7
B♭
D7
lies.
Blue,
G9
C7
oh, so lone-some for you.
Why can't you be
F7
B♭
A
B♭
B
C7
blue o-ver me?
Why can't you be
F7
B♭
blue o-ver me?
rit.

BLUE EYES CRYING IN THE RAIN

Words and Music by
FRED ROSE

kissed good - bye and part - ed I
see her star in heav - en
C7
F
Bb
knew we'd nev - er meet a - gain
blue eyes cry - ing in the rain
F
F7
Bb
Love is like a dy - ing
Some - day when we meet up
F
em - ber On - ly
yon - der We'll stroll

C7
mem - o - ries re - main
hand in hand a - gain
F
Through the ag - es I'll re - mem - ber
In a land that knows no part - ing
C7
blue eyes cry - ing in the
blue eyes cry - ing in the
1 F
Bb
F
rain.
2 F
rain.

BONAPARTE'S RETREAT

Words and Music by REDD STEWART
and PEE WEE KING

girl I ev - er did see So I took her in my arms and
G7
C
told her of her man - y charms I kissed her while the
G7
C
C7
fid - dles played the Bon - a-parte's Re - treat. All the world was
bright as I held her on that night And I heard her

say, "Please don't ev - er go a - way"
C
G7
So I held her in my arms and told her of her
man - y charms, I kissed her while the fid - dles played the
C
1 G7
C
G7
2 G7
C
Bon - a-parte's Re - treat. Met the Bon - a-parte's Re - treat.

BLUE MOON OF KENTUCKY

Words and Music by
BILL MONROE

G
G7
C
moon keep _ on a - shin - in' bright, _ you're gon - na bring-a me back - a my
Cm6
G
Gdim
D7
G
ba - by to - night; _ blue moon keep a - shin - in' bright! ___
D7
G
G7
C7
___ I said blue moon of Ken - tuck - y, to keep on shin - ing, ___
G
D7
___ shine on the one that's gone and left me blue. __

G
G7
I said blue moon of Ken - tuck - y to keep on
C7
G
shin - ing, shine on the one that's
D7
G
G7
gone and left me blue. Well, it was
C
C7
G
G7
on one moon - light night, stars shin - in' bright,

C
C7
G
whis - per on high
love said good -
D7
G
G7
C7
bye; blue moon of Ken - tuck - y, keep on shin - ing,
G
Gdim
D7
shine on the one that's gone and left me blue.
1
G
A7
D7
I said blue
2
G
C7
C#dim
G

BOOT SCOOTIN' BOOGIE

Words and Music by
RONNIE DUNN

E
night when the sun goes down. They got whis-
and let the hors-es run. I go fly-
(Solo)
hot-ter than the Fourth of Ju-ly. I see out-
3
B
-key, wom-en, mu-sic and smoke. It's
in' down that high-way to that hide-a-way
(Solo)
-laws, in-laws, crooks and straights
where all the cow-boy folk go to boot scoot-in'
stuck out in the woods, to do the boot scoot-in'
(Solo)
all out mak-in' it shake do-in' the boot scoot-in'
E
1, 3
2, 4
boo-gie. I've
boo-gie. Yeah,
(Solo)
boo-gie. (Solo ends) The

A
heel to toe, do - cie doe, come on ba - by, let's go
E
boot scoot-in'!
Woh, _
A
Cad - il - lac, Black - jack,
ba - by meet me out back, we're gon - na boo - gie.
E
Oh, _
B7
get down turn a - round, _ go to town, _ boot scoot-in'

E
1
2
D.S.
boo - gie.
Woh,
3
B7
I said, get down, turn a - round, go to town, boot scoot-in'
E
B7
boo - gie. Woh, get down, turn a - round,
N.C.
E
A
E
go to town, boot scoot-in' boo - gie.

BORN TO LOSE

Words and Music by
TED DAFFAN

C
Gm7
3fr
C7
F
life I've al - ways been so blue.
all the hap - pi - ness I knew.
G7/D
Dm7
G7
Born to lose, and now I'm los - in'
Born to lose, and now I'm los - in'
C
E♭dim7
G7sus/D
G7/D
F/G
G7
C
you. Born to lose, it
you. There's no use to
F
G7
C
C7
seems so hard to bear, how I
dream of hap - pi - ness, all I

F
C
G7/D
long to al - ways have you near.
see is on - ly lone - li - ness.
C
G7
C
Gm7
C7
You've grown tired and now you say we're
All my life I've al - ways been so
F
G7/D
Dm7
G7
through.
blue.
Born to lose, and now I'm los - in'
1
C
E♭dim
G7sus/D
G7/D
F/G
G7
2
C
A♭7
C
you.
Born to you.

BY THE TIME I GET TO PHOENIX

Words and Music by
JIMMY WEBB

Fmaj7
Dm7/G
And she'll laugh when she reads the part that says I'm
But she'll just hear that phone keep on
And she'll cry just to think I'd real - ly
Em7
Am7
To Coda
1 Dm7
leav - in', 'cause I've left that girl
ring - in' off the
leave her, though
B♭
G
so man - y times be - fore. By the
2 Dm7
B♭
G
D.S. al Coda
wall, that's all. By the

CODA
Dm7
G7
Cmaj7
time and time
I've tried to tell her so.
Fmaj7
Dm7
E7
Oh, she just did - n't know
I would real - ly
Asus2
G6/9
Asus
go,
I would real - ly go.
G6/9
Asus2
G6/9
Repeat and Fade

BREATHE

Words and Music by HOLLY LAMAR
and STEPHANIE BENTLEY

G/B
C
gets me that way.
Am7
G/B
C
G/B
I watch the sun - light dance a - cross your face and I
Am7
D
nev - er been this swept a - way.
Am7
G/B
All my thoughts just seem to set - tle on
In a way I know my heart is wak -

C
G/B
Am7(add4)
the breeze
when I'm ly - in' wrapped
- ing up
as all the walls
G/B
C
C(add9)
Am7
up in your arms.
The whole world just
come tum - bling down.
Clos - er than I've
G/B
C
G/B
Am7
fades a - way, the on - ly thing I hear is the
ev - er felt be - fore, and I know and you know there's no
Dsus
D
beat - ing of your heart.
need for words right now.
'Cause I can feel you

G Am7 C

breathe, it's wash - ing o - ver me, and sud - den - ly I'm melt - ing in - to you.

D G Am7

There's noth - ing left to prove, ba - by, all we need is just to be

C D 𝄋 G

caught up in the touch, the slow and stead - y

Am7 C G/B

rush. Ba - by, is - n't that the way that love's sup - posed

Am7
Am7(add4)
C/D
D7
To Coda
to be?
I can feel you
C
G/B
Am7
D
breathe,
Just
G
Am7
C
D
breathe.
G
Am7
C
1
D

2
D
D.S. al Coda
Caught up in the
CODA
C
G/B
breathe.
Am7
D
G
Am7
C
Just breathe.
G/B
Am7
G/B
C
I can feel the mag - ic float - ing in the air.
G/B
Am7
G/B
C(add2)
Be - in' with you gets me that way.
rit.

THE CHAIR

Words and Music by HANK COCHRAN
and DEAN DILLON

Gsus2
G
Gsus
G
Am7
- sually packed here on Fri - day nights.
C/D
D7
Oh, if you don't mind, could I talk you out of a light.
G
Gsus2
G
Well, thank you, could I
Gsus2
G
Am
D7
drink you a buy?
Oh, lis - ten to me. What I mean

Am7
D7
G
is can I buy you a drink?
An - y - thing you please.
Am
D7
Gsus2
G
Gsus
G
Oh, you're wel - come. Well, I don't think I caught your name.
Am
C
Bm
Are you wait - ing for some - one to meet
Am
E7/G#
Am
D7
G
you here? Well, that makes two of us; glad you came.

Am7
C/D
No, I don't know the name of the band, but they're good aren't
G
Am7
they? Would you like to dance?
Yeah, I like the song too, it re - minds
C/D
G
me of you and me, ba - by. Do you think there's a chance that
Am
D7
G
G/F#
lat - er on I could drive you home? No, I don't mind at all.

Em
C
Bm
Am
E7/G♯
Oh, I like you too, and to tell you the truth that
Am
D7
Gsus2
G
Am/G
G
was - n't my chair af - ter all. Oh,
C
Bm
Am
E7/G♯
Am
D7
I like you too, and to tell you the truth that was - n't my chair af - ter all.
Gsus2
G
Am/G
G
rit.

COLD, COLD HEART

Words and Music by
HANK WILLIAMS

Moderately

mf

rit.

F

I tried so hard, my Dear, to show that
nev - er know how much it hurts to

a tempo

C7

You're my ev - 'ry dream Yet you're a - fraid each
see you sit and cry You know you need and

F

thing I do is just some e - vil scheme A mem - 'ry from your
want my love yet you're a - fraid to try Why do you run and

F7
B♭
lone - some past keeps us so far a - part Why
hide from life? To try it just ain't smart Why
C7
can't I free your doubt - ful mind and melt your Cold, Cold
can't I free your doubt - ful mind and melt your Cold, Cold
F
Heart An - oth - er love be - fore my time made your heart sad and
Heart There was a time when I be lieved that you be - longed to
C7
blue And so my heart is pay - ing now for
me But now I know your heart is shack - led

F
things I did - n't do . In an - ger, un - kind
to a mem - o - ry The more I learn to
F7
Bb
words are said that make the tear - drops start Why
care for you the more we drift a - part Why
C7
1
can't I free your doubt - ful mind and melt your Cold, Cold
can't I free your doubt - ful mind and
F
2
F
Heart. You'll melt your Cold, Cold Heart.

CHATTAHOOCHEE

Words and Music by JIM McBRIDE
and ALAN JACKSON

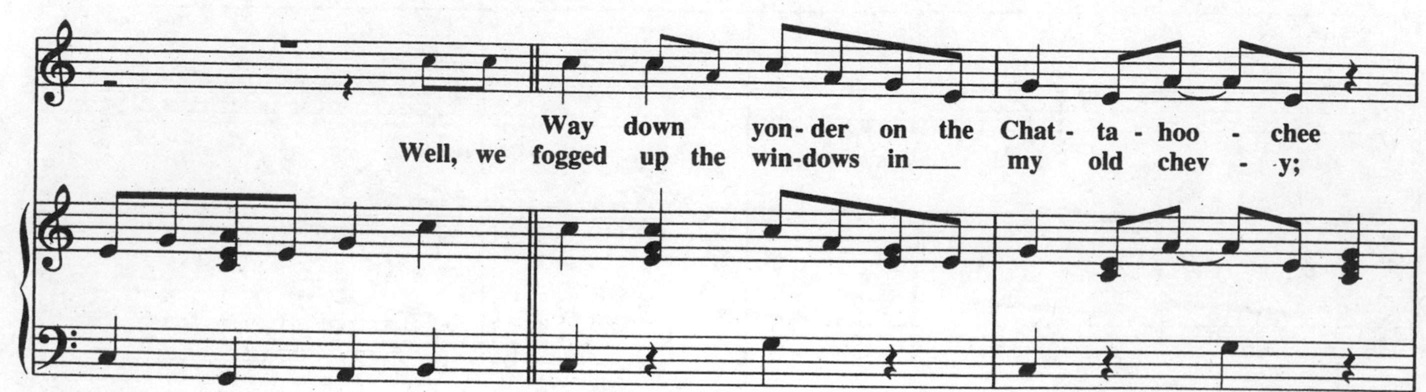

G
C
it gets hot - ter than a hoo-chie coo - chie. We laid rub - ber on the
I was will - in' but __ she was-n't read-y. So, I set-tled for a bur-ger and a
G
C
Geor - gia as - phalt. Got a lit - tle cra - zy but we nev - er got caught.
grape sno - cone. __ I dropped her off __ ear - ly but I did - n't go home.
F
C
1., 2. Down by the riv - er on a Fri - day night, __ pyr - a - mid of cans in the
D.S. Instrumental solo
G
C
F
pale moon - light, talk - ing 'bout cars and dream - in' 'bout wom - en.

D7
G
Nev - er had a plan; just a liv - in' for the min - ute.
Solo ends
Yeah,
C
way down yon - der on the Chat - ta - hoo - chee; nev - er knew how much that mud - dy wa - ter
G
C
To Coda
meant to me. But I learned how to swim and I learned who I was; a lot a - bout liv - in' and a
1
2
D.S. al Coda
G
C
lit - tle 'bout love.
lit - tle 'bout love.
CODA
lit - tle 'bout love, a

G
C
no chord
lot a-bout liv-in' and a lit-tle 'bout love.
rit.
a tempo
C
G
C
G
C

COUNTRY SUNSHINE

Words and Music by DOTTIE WEST,
BILL DAVIS and DIANNE WHILES

G D G G7 C

sun - shine. I was raised on coun - try sun - shine. I'm hap - py with the sim - ple things.

A A7 D

A Sat - ur - day night dance, a pic - ture show and the joy that the blue - bird brings.

G G7 C

I love you please be - lieve me I would - n't want you to ev - er leave

D To Coda G

me, but I was raised on coun - try sun - shine. There's just

D7
G
A
some - thin' 'bout the morn - in' that makes each day a joy to see, and night time brings a
D7
D.S. al Coda
peace-ful feel - in' stretched in - side _ of me. I
CODA
G
sun - shine.
D6
G
G7
C
Yes, you love me and it's in - vit - in' to go where life is more ex -
C
D
G
G7
Repeat and Fade
cit - in', but I was raised _ on coun - try sun - shine. Mm mm

DOWN AT THE TWIST AND SHOUT

Words and Music by
MARY CHAPIN CARPENTER

D
E
find _ my feet out in the mid - dle of a big dance floor. When I
A
hear that fid - dle, wan - na beg for more. Wan - na
E
A
dance to a band from a - Loui - si - an' ___ to - night. ___
E
And I nev - er have _ wan-dered down to New Or - leans, ___
al - li - ga - tor stew and a craw - fish pie, a
ma - ma, bring your pa - pa, bring your sis - ter too. ___ They got

A
nev - er have drift - ed down a bay - ou stream. But I
gulf storm blow - in' in - to town to - night.
lots of mu - sic and lots of room. When they
E
heard that mu - sic on the ra - di - o, and I
Liv - in' on the del - ta it's quite a show. They got hur -
play you a waltz from a nine - teen ten, you're
A
F#m
swore some - day I was gon - na go: down a - high - way 10, past a -
- ri - cane par - ties ev - 'ry time it blows. But here up north it's a
gon - na feel a lit - tle bit young a - gain. Well you learn to dance with your

B7
La - fay-ette; there's a Bat - on Rouge. And I
cold, cold rain, and there ain't no cure for my
rock - in' roll, you learn to swing with
E
won't for-get to send you a card with my re-grets 'cause I'm
blues to-day; ex-cept when the pa-per says Beou - so-leil is a
do - si - do. But you learn to love at the fais do do when you
A
nev-er gon-na come back home.
com-in' in-to town. Ba-by, let's go down. It's
hear a lit-tle Jolie Blon.
D
Sat-ur-day night and the moon is out. I wan-na

A
E
head on o - ver to the Twist and Shout, find a two - step part - ner and a
A
ca - jun beat. When it lifts me up, I'm gon - na
D
E
find __ my feet out in the mid - dle of a big dance flloor. When I
A
E
hear that fid - dle, wan - na beg for more. Wan - na dance to a band from a -

A
Loui - si - an' to - night.
Whoo!
Hey!
D
A
Instrumental solo
E
A
1
2
To Coda
Solo ends
They got a
Solo ends
Bring your
D.S. al Coda

CODA
D
E
A
E
A
D
D7
D

COWBOY TAKE ME AWAY

Words and Music by MARTIE SEIDEL
and MARCUS HUMMON

Original key: F# major. This edition has been transposed up one half-step to be more playable.

Em D/F# G C D
grow some - thing wild and un - rul - y. I wan - na
Em D/F# G Em D/F# G
sleep on the hard ground in the com - fort of your arms on a
Em D/F# G C D
pil - low of blue bon - nets and a blan - ket made of stars. Oh, it
C G/B D
sounds good to me. I said, cow - boy,

G
G/B
Am7
D/B
7 fr
D
take me a - way. Fly this girl as high
Em
C
D
as you can in - to the wild blue. Set me
G
G/B
Am7
D/B
7 fr
D
free, oh, I pray, clos - er to
Em
C
D
heav-en a - bove and clos - er to you, clos - er to you.

C
G/B
G
C
G/B
G
C
G/B
G
Em
D
Em
D/F#
G
I wan-na walk and not run.
I wan-na
Em
D/F#
G
Em
D/F#
G
C
skip and not fall.
I wan-na look at the ho-ri-zon and not see
D
Em
D/F#
G
a build-ing stand-in' tall.
I wan-na be the on-ly one
for

Em
D/F#
G
Em
D/F#
G
C
miles and miles ex - cept for may - be you and your
D
C
G/B
D
sim-ple smile. Oh, it sounds good to me. Yes, it sounds
C
G/B
D
G
G/B
Am7
D/B
7 fr
so good to me. Cow-boy, take me a - way.
D
Em
C
Fly this girl as high as you can in - to the wild blue.

D
G
G/B
Am7
D/B
7 fr
Set me free, oh, I pray,
D
Em
C
clos - er to heav-en a - bove and clos - er to you,
D/F#
D
G
G/B
Am7
C
To Coda
clos - er to you.
D
Em
C

D/F# D G G/B Am7 G/B D

Em C D/F# D

I said_ I wan-na

Em D/F# G Em D/F# G

touch the earth,_ I wan-na break it in_ my hands._ I wan-na

Em D/F# G C D

D.S. al Coda

grow some - thing wild_ and un - rul - y. Oh, it sounds_

CODA
G
G/B
G/A
G/B
D
Clos - er to you.
D
G
G/B
Am
D/B
7fr
D
Cow - boy, take me a - way,
clos - er to you.
Em
C
D
G
G/B
Am7
G/B
Instrumental ad lib.
D
Em
C
1-3
D
4
D

CRYIN' TIME

Words and Music by
BUCK OWENS

G
G7
C
eyes; I can tell___ by the way you___ hold me dar - lin' That it
G
D7
G
Fine
won't be long be - fore it's___ cry - in' time. Now you said that you've___ some - one___ you love
D7
G
bet - ter___ That's the way it's hap - pened ev - 'ry time be - fore, And as
G7
C
G
D7
G
D.S. al Fine
sure___ as the sun comes up to - mor - row___ Cry - in' time will start when you walk___ out the door. Oh, it's

DANG ME

Words and Music by
ROGER MILLER

CHORUS
Bb
C7
F
F7
Dang me, dang me, they ought-ta take a rope and hang me high from the high - est
Bb
Guitar Tacet
F
To Coda
1
tree, wom-an, would you weep for me!
2
D.S. al Coda
(Spoken) They say
CODA
F
F/C
F7
Bb
C7
F

DEEP IN THE HEART OF TEXAS

Words by JUNE HERSHEY
Music by DON SWANDER

B♭/D
C7
land I un - der - stand, and it's
F
F7/E♭
B♭/D
G9
C7
E♭7
C7
there I long to be. The
F6
stars at night are big and
coy - otes wail a - long the
bright, deep in the heart of
trail, deep in the heart of
(Clap Clap Clap Clap)

C7
Tex - as; The prai - rie
Tex - as; The rab - bits
sky is wide and high,
rush a - round the brush,
(Clap Clap Clap
Clap)
deep in the heart of Tex - as.
deep in the heart of Tex - as.
F
F6
The sage in bloom is like per -
The cow - boys cry, "Ki - yip - pee -

C7
fume, deep in the heart of Tex - as;
yi," deep in the heart of Tex - as;
(Clap Clap Clap Clap)
Re - minds me of the
The dog - ies bawl, and
one I love, deep in the heart of
bawl and bawl, deep in the heart of
(Clap Clap Clap Clap)
1 F Gm7 C7
2 F B♭6 F
Tex - as. The Tex - as.
8vb

ELVIRA

Words and Music by
DALLAS FRAZIER

G7
girl can sho' nuff make my lit-'tle light shine
C
F7
C7
I get a fun-ny feel-ing Up and down my spine 'Cause I know that
G7
C7
my El-vir-a's mine I'm sing-in' El-vir-a,
El-vir-a, My heart's on

Verse 2. Tonight I'm gonna meet her
At the hungry house cafe
And I'm gonna give her all the love I can
She's gonna jump and holler
'Cause I saved up my last two dollar
And we're gonna search and find that preacher man
Chorus

FOR THE GOOD TIMES

Words and Music by
KRIS KRISTOFFERSON

C7
C7sus
F
F6
Fmaj7
F
F7
time to spend to - geth - er. There's no
mor - row or for - ev - er. There'll be
Bb
Gm
Gm7
C7sus
C7
need to watch the bridg - es that we're burn - ing.
time e - nough for sad - ness when you leave me.
Guitar Tacet
F
Lay your head up - on my
C7
pil - low, Hold your warm and ten - der

F
Gm7
C7
F
Fmaj7
bod - y close to mine.
Hear the whis - per of the
F7
Bb
Bbm
rain - drops blow - ing soft a - gainst the win - dow
C7
Gm
C7sus
C7
And make be - lieve you love me one more time
For the
1
F
F6
Fmaj7
F6
good times.
I'll get a -
2
F
Bb6
F
good times.

FRIENDS IN LOW PLACES

Words and Music by DEWAYNE BLACKWELL
and EARL BUD LEE

A
last one to show; I was the last one you thought you'd see
just say good - night and I'll show my - self to the door.
there.
And I saw the sur - prise and the
Hey, I did - n't mean to
B♭dim7
Bm7
2fr
fear in his eyes when I took his glass of cham - pagne.
cause a big scene, just give me an ho - ur and
Bm7♭5/D
E
And I toast - ed you, said, "Hon - ey,
then, well, I'll be as high as that i -

we may be through,
but you'll nev - er hear me com - plain."
- vo - ry tow - er that you're liv - in' in.
A
'Cause I've got friends in low plac - es where the
whis - key drowns and the beer chas - es my blues
Bm7
2fr
a - way,
E
and I'll be o - kay.

A
Yeah, I'm not big on so - cial grac - es. Think I'll
slip on down to the o - a - sis. Oh,
Bm7
2fr
E
A
To Coda
I've got friends in low plac - es.

Bm7
2fr
E
A
D.S. al Coda
Well, I
CODA
I've got friends_ in low plac - es where the
whis - key ___ drowns ___ and the beer ___ chas - es my blues ___

Bm7
2fr
E
a - way,
and I'll
be o - kay.
A
Yeah,
I'm not
big
on
so - cial grac - es. Think I'll
slip on
down
to the
o - a - sis. Oh,
I've got
friends
in low
plac - es.
Repeat and Fade
Optional Ending

GALVESTON

Words and Music by
JIM WEBB

B♭
Dm/A
Gm7
C
Dm
B♭/C
glow - ing.
She was twen - ty
one,
when
flash - in'.
I clean my
gun,
and
B♭
B♭/C
1
F
B♭
C
I left Gal - ves - ton.
dream of Gal - ves - ton.
2
F
B♭
F
A♭
B♭
I still see her
stand - ing
by
the wa -
A♭
B♭
Cm
- ter,
stand - ing there

Ab
4fr
Fm
Bb7
look - ing out to sea. And is she wait - ing there for
Eb
3fr
Gm
3fr
Cm
3fr
Db
me, on the beach where we used to run?
Bb
C
F
Bb
C
Gal - ves - ton, oh! Gal - ves - ton,
F
Fmaj7
F7
I am so a - fraid of

B♭
Dm/A
Gm7
3fr
C
F
dy - ing,
be - fore I dry
the tears she's
B♭
Dm/A
Gm7
3fr
C
Dm
F/C
cry - ing,
be - fore I watch
your sea birds
B♭
Am
Gm7
3fr
C
fly - ing in the sun
at Gal - ves - ton,
D
C
D
at Gal - ves - ton.

GAMES PEOPLE PLAY

Words and Music by
JOE SOUTH

C
in their i - vo - ry tow - ers, 'til they're cov - ered up with
So, we gaze at an eight by ten, think - in' 'bout the things that
read your hor - o - scopre, cheat your fate, and fur - ther - more, to
for your pride and your van - i - ty. Turn your back on hu -
B♭
C
F
flow - ers, in the back of a black lim - ou - sine.
might have been. It's a dir - ty rot - ten shame.
hell with hate. Come on get on board.
man - i - ty. and you don't give a da, da, da, da, da.
La, da, da, da,
F
C
B♭
da, da, da. La, da, da, da, da, da, dee. Talk - in' 'bout you and me,
C
F
1-3
4
D.S. and Fade
and the games peo - ple play.
Oh, we make one an -
Peo - ple walk - in' up
Look a - round, tell me
La, da da, da,

GENTLE ON MY MIND

Words and Music by
JOHN HARTFORD

GRANDPA
(Tell Me 'Bout the Good Old Days)

Words and Music by
JAMIE O'HARA

A
D
zy.
Grand - pa,
And Grand - pa,
G
take me back to yes - ter - day
let's wan - der back in - to the past,
when the line be - tween
then paint me the
D
A7
D
right and wrong
pic - ture
did - n't seem so haz - y.
of long a - go.
G
Did lov - ers real - ly fall in love to stay,
and stand be - side each

D
A7
oth - er come what may. Was a prom - ise real - ly some - thing peo - ple kept,
D
not just some - thing they would say? (and then for - get) Did fam - 'lies real - ly
G
D
bow their heads to pray? Did dad - dies real - ly nev - er go a - way?
Em
G/A
Oh, oh, grand - pa, tell me 'bout the good old days.

1.
D
2.
D
Oh, oh,
Em
G/A
D
grand - pa, tell me 'bout the good old days.
G
D
A7
D
D.S. and Fade
Did fam - 'lies real - ly

THE GREATEST MAN I NEVER KNEW

Words and Music by RICHARD LEIGH
and LAYNG MARTINE, JR.

F C Am F G7

and ev - 'ry day we said ___ hel - lo ___
He nev - er had too much ___ to say. ___
The man I thought could nev - er die ___

C Am F G Am

but nev - er touched at all. ___ He was in his pa -
Too much was on his mind. ___ I nev - er real - ly knew
has been dead al - most a year. ___ Oh, he was good at bus -

Em F Esus E

- per. I was in my ___ room.
___ him, oh, and now it seems so ___ sad.
- 'ness but there was bus - 'ness left ___ to ___ do.

F G7

To Coda

How was I to know ___ he thought I hung the ___ moon?
Ev - 'ry - thing he gave ___ to us took all he ___ had. ___
He nev - er said he loved ___ me. Guess he

1 C
2 C
Em
Then the days
F
C
G
C
turned in - to years, _ and the mem-'ries to black _ and white. _
Em
F
C
He grew cold like an old ___ win - ter wind ___ blow-ing a - cross ___ my life. _
G7sus
G7
D.S. al Coda
CODA
F
G
C
thought I ___ knew. _

GREEN GREEN GRASS OF HOME

Words and Music by
CURLY PUTMAN

D
D7
G
pa - pa.
play on.
Down the road I look and
Down the lane I walk with
For there's a guard and there's a
G7
C
Cdim
C
Bm
Am
there runs Ma - ry,
my sweet Ma - ry,
sad old padre,
hair of gold and lips like cher - ries. It's
hair of gold and lips like cher - ries. It's
arm in arm we'll walk at day - break. A -
G
D7
Am7
D7
G
C
good to touch the green, green grass of home.
good to touch the green, green grass of home.
gain I'll touch the green, green grass of home.
3
G
G7
Yes, they'll all come to meet me, arms
Yes, they'll all come to meet me. arms
Yes, they'll all come to see me in the

HALF AS MUCH

Words and Music by
CURLEY WILLIAMS

D
D7
G
me when there's no one else a - round.
E7
You on - ly build me up to let me
A7
D
down. If you missed me
half as much as I miss you, you would - n't

A7
stay a - way half as much as you do.
D
D7
G
I know that I would nev - er be this blue.
A7
If you on - ly loved me half as much as I love
1
D
you.
If you
2
D
A7
D
you.
8vb

HAPPY TRAILS

from the Television Series THE ROY ROGERS SHOW

Words and Music by
DALE EVANS

E♭
3fr
E♭
3fr
hap - py one for you. Hap - py trails to
Edim7
you un - til we meet a -
B♭7
B♭7sus
B♭7
gain. Hap - py trails to you, keep
B♭7♯5
E♭(add9)
E♭
3fr
smil - in' un - til then. Who

Eb7
Abmaj7
Ab6
3fr
cares a - bout the clouds when we're to - geth - er? Just
C7
F9
Bb7
sing a song and bring the sun - ny weath - er. Hap - py
Eb
3fr
Bbm6
6fr
C7
Fm
Bb7
trails to you till we meet a -
1
Eb
3fr
Bb7
2
Eb
3fr
Ab
4fr
Eb6
gain. Hap - py gain.

HARD ROCK BOTTOM OF YOUR HEART

Words and Music by
HUGH PRESTWOOD

B
A
let your love down, I have
on sol - id ground. Do we
E
B
A
prayed that with time and com - pas - sion,
roll up our sleeves and re - pair it,
F♯m
A
B
you'd come a - round.
or burn it down?
E
A
And I keep wait - ing for you to for - give

B
E
me.
And you keep
say - ing
you
A
B
can't
e - ven
start.
And I
E
A
E
feel
like
a
stone
you
have
picked
up
and
B
A
thrown
to the hard
rock
bot -

B
E
tom of your heart,
to the hard
A
B
E
To Coda
1
rock bot - tom of your heart.
Now this home
2
Bm
A
Bm
We can't just block it out.
We've got to
A
Bm
A
talk it out
un - til our hearts get back in

E
Bm7
2fr
touch.
I need your
E
Bm7
2fr
E
love, I miss it.
I can't go on like this, it
F#m
A
B
hurts too much.
E
A
B
(Instrumental solo)

E
A
B
D.S. al Coda
(Solo ends) And I keep
CODA
A
B
To the hard rock bot - tom of your heart,
E
A
to the hard rock bot -
B
E
- tom of your heart.

A
B
E
A
B
E
A
E/B
B
Whoo,
whoo,
E
A
B
Repeat and Fade
whoo.

HELP ME MAKE IT THROUGH THE NIGHT

Words and Music by
KRIS KRISTOFFERSON

A7
To Coda
1
skin.
time.
lone.
Like the shad - ows on the
D
G
2
wall.
Help me make it thru the
D
G
D
night.
I don't care who's right or
G
wrong,
I don't try to un - der -

D
stand.
Let the dev - il take to -
E7
mor - row.
Lord, to - night I need a
A7
D.S. al Coda
friend.
CODA
Help me
D
G
D
make it thru the night.

HERE'S A QUARTER
(Call Someone Who Cares)

Words and Music by
TRAVIS TRITT

D
lone - some and scared.
me un - a - ware.
G
And you say you'd be
But the fact is you've
C
hap - py if you could just come back
run. Girl, that can't be un - done.
G
home. Well, here's a quar - ter. Call
So here's a quar - ter. Call

D
G
some - one who cares.
some - one who cares.
G7
C
Call some - one who'll listen and
G
might give a damn. May - be
D
one of your sor - did af - fairs.

D7
G
But don't you come a - round here
G7/B
C
hand - ing me none of your lines.
G
Here's a quar - ter. Call
D
To Coda
G
some - one who cares.

G7
C
G
D
D9
Bm/E
D9/F#
G
G7/B
C
G

D G

D.S. al Coda

Girl, I

CODA

G C7

Yeah, here's a

G D C7

quar - ter. Call some - one who cares.

G G7

Yeah, yeah.

rit.

HEY, GOOD LOOKIN'

Words and Music by
HANK WILLIAMS

ba - by, Don't you think may - be
look - in', I know I've been took - en
D7
G7
C
We could find us a brand new rec - i - pe
How's a - bout keep - in' stead - y com - pa - ny
C7
F
C
I got a hot rod Ford and a two dol - lar bill and
I'm gon - na throw my date book o - ver the fence and
F
C
F
I know a spot right o - ver the hill There's so - da pop and the
find me one for five or ten cents I'll keep it 'til it's

D7
G7
danc - in's free, so if you wan-na have fun come a - long with me
cov-ered with age 'Cause I'm writ - in' your name down on ev - 'ry page
f
C
Hey, Good Look-in' What - cha got cook-in'
Hey, Good Look-in' What - cha got cook-in'
D7
G7
1
C
How's a-bout cook - in' some - thin' up with me.
How's a-bout cook - in' some - thin' up with
2
C
F
C
I'm me.

I CAN LOVE YOU LIKE THAT

Words and Music by MARIBETH DERRY,
JENNIFER KIMBALL and STEVE DIAMOND

C
Em
like ro - man - tic mov - ies; you nev - er will __ for - get the
I'm no Ca - sa - no - va, but I swear this much is true:
F
G7sus
Em7
way you felt when Ro - me - o kissed Ju - li - et. __ All this time that you've been wait -
I'll be hold - ing noth - ing back when it comes to you. You dream of love that's ev - er - last -
F
Em7
F
- ing, you don't have to wait no ______ more.
- ing. Well, ba - by, o - pen up your ______ eyes.
G7sus
C
Em
I can love you like that. I would make you my world, _ move heav - en and earth _

F
G7sus
if you were my girl.
I will give you my heart,
C
Em
F
be all that you need,
show you you're ev - 'ry-thing that's pre-cious to me.
B♭
G7sus
If you give me a chance,
I can love you like that.
1 C
F
G7sus
I

2
C
Gm7
3fr
You want ten - der - ness, I got ten -
Dm7
C
- der - ness. And I see through _ to the
Gm7
3fr
Dm7
heart of you. _ If you want a man who un - der - stands, _
F
G7sus
you don't have to look ver - y far. _

G
C
I can love you, I can, I can love you like that.
I would make you my world,
Em
F
move heav - en and earth if you were my girl.
G7sus
C
Em
I will give you my heart, be all that you need, show you you're ev -
Repeat and Fade
F
G7sus
'ry - thing that's pre-cious to me. I can love you like that.

I CAN'T STOP LOVING YOU

Words and Music by
DON GIBSON

C
C7
F
time heals a bro - ken heart,
C
G7
but time has stood still since we've been a -
C
F/G
C
C7
F
part.
I can't stop lov - ing you,
I can't stop lov - ing you,
C
3
so I've made up my mind to live in
there's no use to try. Pre - tend there's
3

G7
C
mem - o - ry of old lone-some times.
some - one new; I can't live a lie.
C7
F
I can't stop want - ing you, it's use - less to
I can't stop want - ing you the way that I
C
G7
say, so I'll just live my life in dreams of yes - ter -
do. There's on - ly been one love for me, that one love is
1
C
F/G
C
G7
2
C
F
C
day. Those hap-py you.
3

(I Never Promised You A)
ROSE GARDEN

Words and Music by
JOE SOUTH

Moderately Bright, with a beat

Am D G

mf

D no chord Am D G

I beg your par - don, I nev - er prom - ised you a rose __ gar - den.

Am D G

A - long with the sun - shine, there's got to be a lit - tle rain_ some - time.

C C+

When you take you got to give, so live and let live __ or let

Am
D
go, oh, oh, oh. I beg your par - don,
G
I nev - er prom - ised you a rose gar - den.
1. I could
2.
3. I could
4.
G
prom - ise you things like big dia - mond rings, but you don't find ros - es
sweet talk - ing you could make it come true I would give you the world right now
sing you a tune and prom - ise you the moon, but if that's what it takes to
look be - fore you leap, still wa - ters run deep and there won't al - ways be

Am
grow - ing on stalks of clo - ver,
on a sil - ver plat - ter,
hold you, I'd just as soon let you go,
some - one there to pull you out,
D
so you bet - ter think it o - ver.
but what would it mat - ter.
but there's one thing I want you to know.
and you know what I'm talk - in' a - bout.
1,3
2,4
Am
2. When it's
4. You better
So smile for a - while and

D
Bdim
let's be jol - ly; love should - n't be so
E
Am
mel - an - chol - y. Come a - long and share the
C
To Coda
good times while we can.
D
D.S. al Coda
I beg your
CODA
D
I beg your

Am
D
par - don,
I nev - er prom - ised you a
G
rose
gar - den.
A - long with the
Am
D
sun - shine,
there's got to be a lit - tle
G
rain
some - time.

I OVERLOOKED AN ORCHID

G7 C G Gdim

blush - in' rose, the rose could not com - pare, But
or - chid, I was look - ing for a rose, And

G D7 G C G

how was such as I to un - der - stand.
now I pay the price with bit - ter tears.

Gdim G G7 C

I O - ver - looked An Or - chid, while search - ing for a

mp-mf

G Gdim G

rose; The or - chid that I o - ver - looked was

D7 D7+5 G

you; The rose that I was

G7 C G Gdim

search - ing for has proved to be un - true; The

G D7 1 G A7

or - chid now I find, my dear, was you.

D7 2 G C G

The you.

poco rit.

I THOUGHT IT WAS YOU

Words and Music by TIM MENSY
and GARY HARRISON

Moderately

D D/F# Gsus2 D/A A

mf

D D/F# Gsus2 A7sus D

I called your name out loud
I still drive by your house

Asus A G Asus A D D/A A

to a stranger yesterday.
takin' trips down memory lane.

D Asus A

When she turned around I said I'm
We had our future worked out, at least we

G
Asus
A
D
sor - ry and just walked a - way.
did on that old porch swing.
G
D
From a dis - tance she had that look
To - day in my rear - view mir - ror
G
D/F♯
Em
and for a sec - ond or two
I saw an old Mal - i - bu
A
D
D/F♯
I thought it was you.
girl, I thought it was you.
It took a mo -

G Asus A D G/B D/A G Asus
-ment to catch my breath, tried to brace my-self. Still don't have a clue
D D/F# G Asus A
how to leave your mem - 'ry be-hind
D G/B D/A G
af - ter all this time. I hear there's
Bm D/A G#m7♭5
one spe-cial love in each life and I must look like a

D/A
A
fool. I thought it was you.
1
D
D/F#
Gsus2
D/A
A
2
D
D/F#
G
G#m7♭5
D/A
A
Am I real - ly a fool? I thought it was you.
D
D/F#
Gsus2
Asus
A
D
D/F#

G
G/A
D
D/F♯
I thought it was you.
Gsus2
A7sus
D
D/F♯
Why could-n't it be you?
G
G/A
A
D
D/F♯
Gsus2
A7sus
A7
D
D/F♯
G
Asus
Repeat and Fade

I WALK THE LINE

Words and Music by
JOHN R. CASH

Moderate

mf

Dm7 Gm7 C7 F6

1. I keep a close watch on this heart of mine.
very easy to be true.

Gm7

I keep my eyes wide open all the
I find myself alone when each day is

F6 F7 B♭ Gm7

time. I keep the ends out for the tie that
through. Yes, I'll admit that I'm a fool for

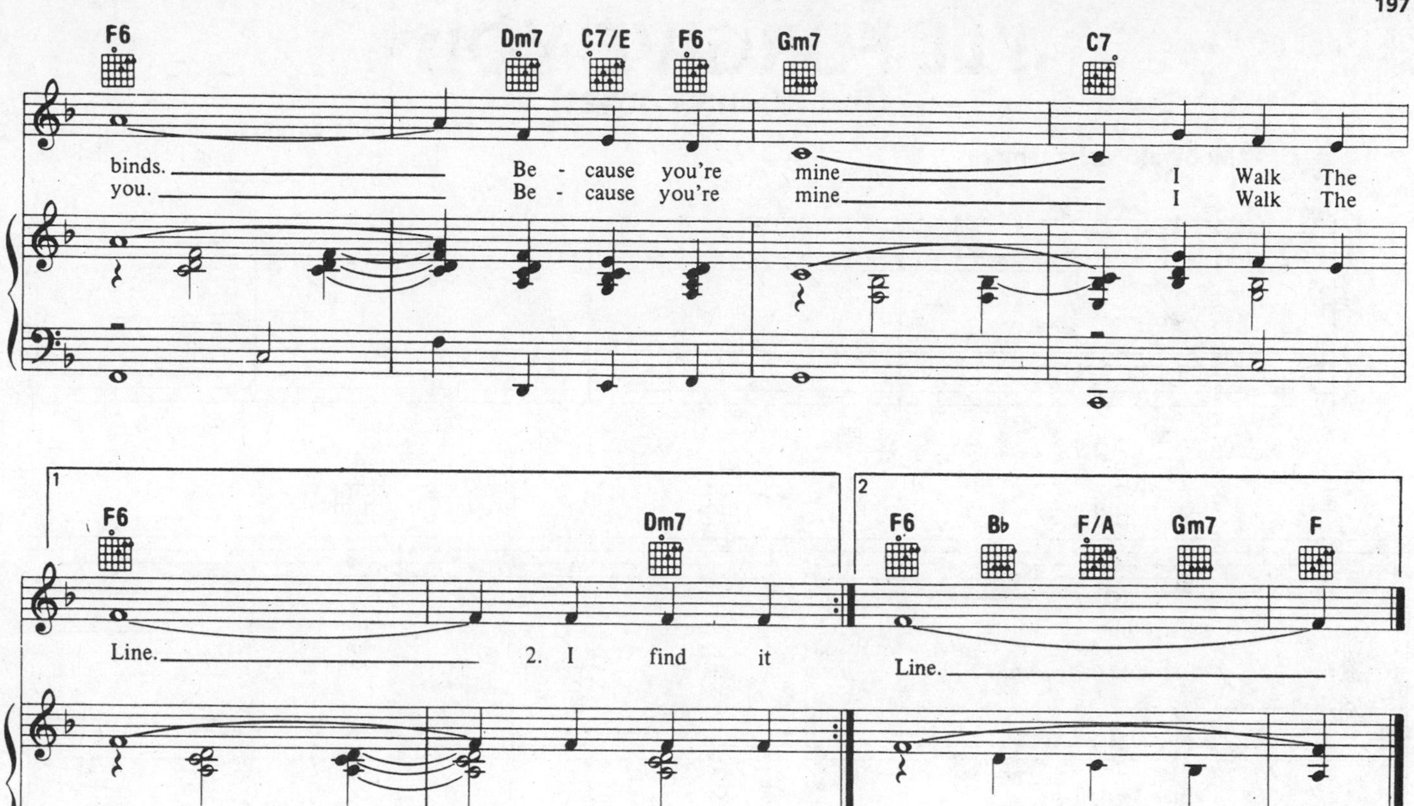

3. As sure as night is dark and day is light,
I keep you on my mind both day and night.
And happiness I've known proves that it's right.
Because you're mine I Walk The Line.

4. You've got a way to keep me on your side.
You give me cause for love that I can't hide.
For you I know I'd even try to turn the tide.
Because you're mine I Walk The Line.

5. I keep a close watch on this heart of mine.
I keep my eyes wide open all the time.
I keep the ends out for the tie that binds.
Because you're mine I Walk The Line.

I'LL FORGIVE YOU
(But I Can't Forget)

Words and Music by J.L. FRANK and PEE WEE KING

Ab Bb7

o'er you; I'll for - give you but
ev - er; I'll for - give you but
out you; I'll for - give you but

Eb Bb7+5

I can't for - get.
I can't for - get.
I can't for - get. You

Eb Bb7 Eb7 Ab

ask me to for - get you, lit - tle dar - ling,

Bb7 Ab/Bb Bb7

To for - get that our plans were up -

Eb
Bb7+5
Eb
Bb7
set; I try, oh, so
Eb7
Ab
hard, not to re - mem - ber; I'll for -
Bb7
1,2 Eb
give you, but I can't for - get.
F9
Bb9+5
3 Eb
Abm
Bb/Eb
Eb
The
Now
get.
mf
mf
ritard.
mp

IF I SAID YOU HAVE A BEAUTIFUL BODY WOULD YOU HOLD IT AGAINST ME

Words and Music by
DAVID BELLAMY

Bb7
Eb
Cm
dy-ing of thirst, would your flow-ing love come quench me?
If I said
Ab
Bb7
Eb
you have a beau-ti-ful bod - y, would you hold it a-gainst me?
VERSE
Eb
Ab
Now, we could talk all night a - bout the weath - er;
Now, rain can fall so soft a - gainst the win - dow;
Fm7
could tell you 'bout my friends out on the
the sun can shine so bright up in the

Bb7
Fm7
Bb
Eb
coast.
sky.
I could ask a lot
But dad - dy al - ways told
Ab
of cra - zy ques - tions,
me, don't make small talk;
he said,
Fm7
Bb7
or ask you what I real - ly want to know.
"Come on out and say what's on your mind."
Eb
D. S. and fade on CHORUS
1.
NC
If I said
2.
NC
So, if I said

I'M ALREADY THERE

Words and Music by RICHIE McDONALD,
FRANK MYERS and GARY BAKER

Bb/D
Abmaj9
4fr
when he heard the sound of the kids laugh - in' in the back - ground he had to
Eb
Ab
4fr
Bbsus
Bb
wipe a - way a tear from his eye. A lit - tle
Cm
Bb/D
voice came on the phone and said, "Dad - dy, when you com - in' home?" He said the
Eb
Fm
Eb/G
3fr
Ab
4fr
Ab/Bb
Bb
first thing that came to his mind: I'm al - read - y there.

E♭
B♭/D
Cm7
B♭
Take a look a - round.
I'm the sun - shine in your hair,
A♭
4fr
E♭
A♭/B♭
B♭
I'm the shad - ow on the ground.
I'm the whis - per in the wind,
E♭
B♭/D
Cm
I'm your i - mag - i - nar - y friend.
And I know
Gm7
A♭
4fr
A♭/B♭
B♭
I'm in your prayers.
Oh, I'm al - read - y there.

Eb(add2)
3fr
Cm7
Ab
4fr
She
Bb/D
Abmaj9
4fr
got back on the phone said, "I real - ly miss you dar - lin'. Don't
Eb
Bbsus
Bb
Ab/C
wor - ry a - bout the kids, they'll be al - right. I wish
Bb/D
Abmaj9
4fr
I was in your arms, ly - in' right there be - side you. But I

E♭
B♭sus
B♭
know that I'll_ be in your dreams_ to - night._ And I'll
Cm
B♭/D
gent - ly kiss your lips,_ touch you with my fin - ger tips._ So, turn
E♭
Fm
E♭/G
3fr
A♭
4fr
A♭/B♭
B♭
out the light and close your eyes._ I'm al - read - y there._
E♭
B♭/D
Cm
B♭
_ Don't make a sound_ I'm the beat of your heart,_

A♭
4fr
E♭
A♭/B♭
I'm the moon - light shin - in' down.
I'm the whis - per in the wind,
E♭
B♭/D
Cm7
and I'll be there till the end.
Can you feel
Gm7
A♭
4fr
B♭sus
B♭
the love that we've shared?
Oh, I'm al - read - y there."
E♭
Fm
E♭/G
3fr
We may be a thou -

A♭
4fr
G♭
D♭/F
- sand miles a - part,
but I'll be with you wher -
B♭sus
B♭
ev - er you are.
I'm al - read - y there.
E♭(add2)
3fr
B♭/D
Cm7
Take a look a - round.
I'm the sun - shine in your hair,
A♭sus2
N.C.
B♭
I'm the shad - ow on the ground.
I'm the whis - per in the wind,

E♭
B♭/D
Cm7
and I'll be there till the end. Can you feel
Gm7
A♭
B♭
the love that we've shared? Oh, I'm al - read - y there.
Cm
B♭
A♭
E♭/G
Fm7
B♭
Yeah, oh, I'm al - read - y
N.C.
E♭(add2)
Cm7
A♭
D♭
E♭
there.
rit.

I'M SO LONESOME I COULD CRY

Words and Music by
HANK WILLIAMS

F
cry. I've nev - er seen a
cry. The si - lence of a
night so long, When time goes crawl - ing
fall - ing star Lights up a pur - ple
F7
Bb
by. The moon just went be -
sky. And as I won - der
F
C7
hind a cloud To hide its face and
where you are I'm So Lone - some I Could
1
F
2
F
cry. Did you Cry.

IF TOMORROW NEVER COMES

Words and Music by KENT BLAZY
and GARTH BROOKS

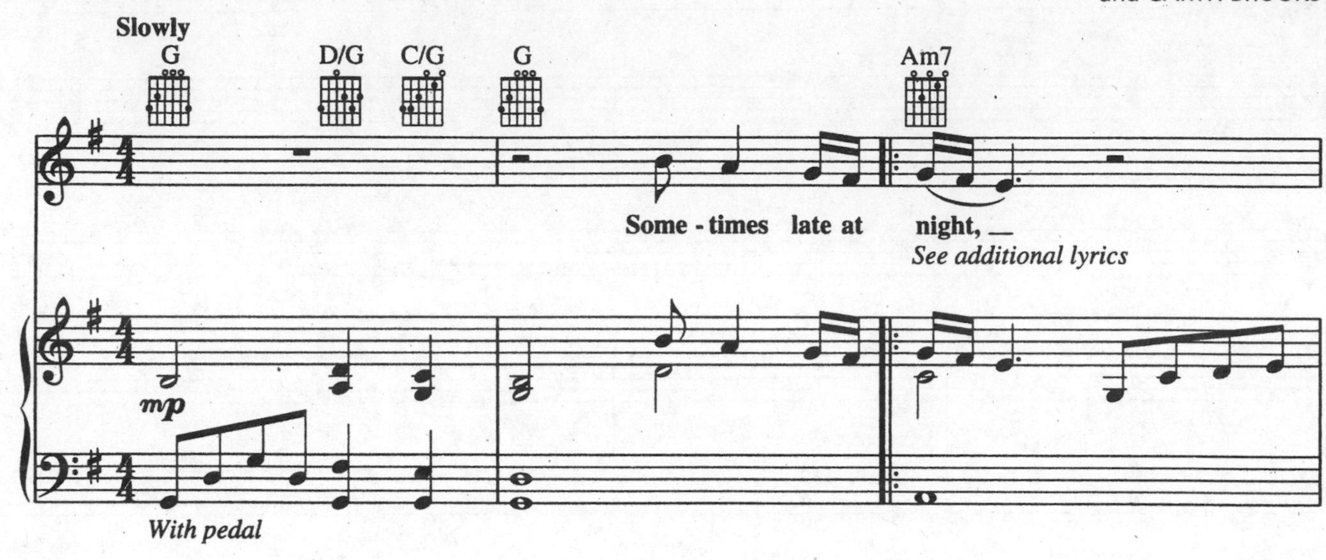

D
C
G
C/G
off the lights and lay there in the dark.
G
Am7
And the thought cross - es my mind,
D
C/G
G
Am/G
G
if I nev - er wake up in the morn - ing,
D
Am7
D
C
would she ev - er doubt the way I feel a - bout her in my

G
C/G
G
heart.
If to mor - row nev - er
C
comes,
will she know how much I
G
loved her?
Did I try in ev - 'ry
D
Am7
D
C
way to show her ev - 'ry - day that she's my on - ly one?

G
Am7
G/B
And if my time on earth were
C
D
through,
and she must face this world with-
Em7
Bm7
Em
out me,
is the love I gave her in the past
Am7
D
gon-na be e-nough to last
if to-mor-row nev-er

Additional Lyrics

2\. 'Cause I've lost loved ones in my life.
Who never knew how much I loved them.
Now I live with the regret
That my true feelings for them never were revealed.
So I made a promise to myself
To say each day how much she means to me
And avoid that circumstance
Where there's no second chance to tell her how I feel. ('Cause)
Chorus

JEALOUS HEART

Words and Music by
JENNY LOU CARSON

G7
her a - way for - ev - er. Jeal - ous
did you make her hate me Now there's
gone and found an - oth - er. Oh, I'll
C
heart, Now I'm the lone - ly one.
noth - ing left but Jeal - ous you.
nev - er see my love a - gain.
C7
F
I was part of ev' - ry - thing she
Man - y times I trust - ed you to
Through the years her mem - o - ry will
C
G7
planned for. And I know she
guide me. But your guid - ing
haunt me. E - ven tho, we're

C C7

loved me at the start. Now she
on - ly brought me tears. Why, oh
man - y miles a - part. It's so

F C

hates the sight of all I stand for.
why must I have you in - side me.
hard to know she'll nev - er want me.

G7

All be - cause of you. Oh jeal - ous
Jeal - ous heart, for all my lone - ly
'Cause she heard your beat - ing jeal - ous

1,2 C 3 C

heart. You have
years. Jeal - ous heart.

IT WASN'T GOD WHO MADE HONKY TONK ANGELS

Words and Music by
J.D. MILLER

Eb
Fm7
Eb
Bb7 Adim
Eb
Eb7
Ab
wife.
blame.
It was - n't God who made honk - y tonk an - gels
Bb7
Eb
Bb7 Adim
As you said in the words of your song;
Too man - y
Eb
Eb7
Ab
Bb7
times mar - ried men think they're still sin - gle;
That has caused man - y a
1
Eb
F7
A
Bb7
2
Eb
Ab
Eb
good girl to go wrong.
It's a
wrong.

THE KEEPER OF THE STARS

Words and Music by KAREN STALEY,
DANNY MAYO and DICKEY LEE

Em
A7sus
A7
D
long be-fore _ we ev - er knew.
just to look _ in - to your eyes.
Now I ____ just
I know_ I
A/C#
Bm
can't ___ be - lieve ___
don't ___ de - serve ___
you're in ___ my
a treas - ure _ like
G
life.
you.
Heav - en's smil - in'
There real - ly ___
D/F#
Em
down on me ___
are no words _
as I look at you ___ to -
to show my grat - i -

A7sus
A7
G
night.
tude.
I tip my
So, I tip my
hat
A
F#m
to the Keep - er of the Stars.
G
Em
He sure knew what he was do - in'
A7
D
when he joined these two hearts.
I hold ev - 'ry -

G
A
thing
when I hold _ you in my
F#m
G
D/F#
arms.
I've got all ___ I'll ev - er
Em
A7
need,
thanks to the Keep - er of ___ the
1
G
D
A7sus
Stars.
2
D
Stars.

A/C#
It was no ac-ci-dent,
Bm
G
me find - ing you.
D/F#
Some-one had a hand in it
Em
A7
D
A7sus
D
long be-fore we ev-er knew.
rit.

LAST DATE

By FLOYD CRAMER

3
3
3
3
3
3
3
3

KING OF THE ROAD

Words and Music by
ROGER MILLER

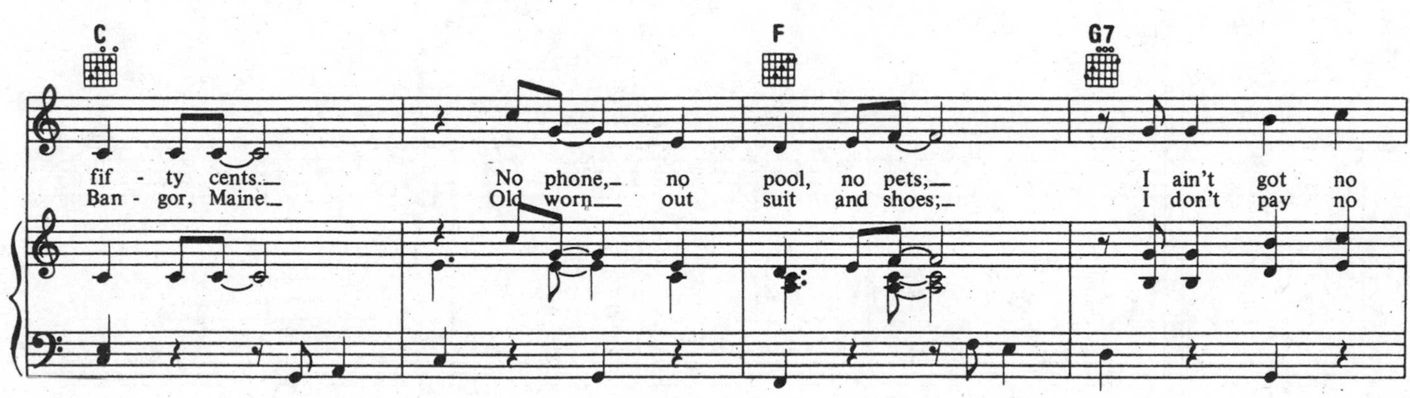

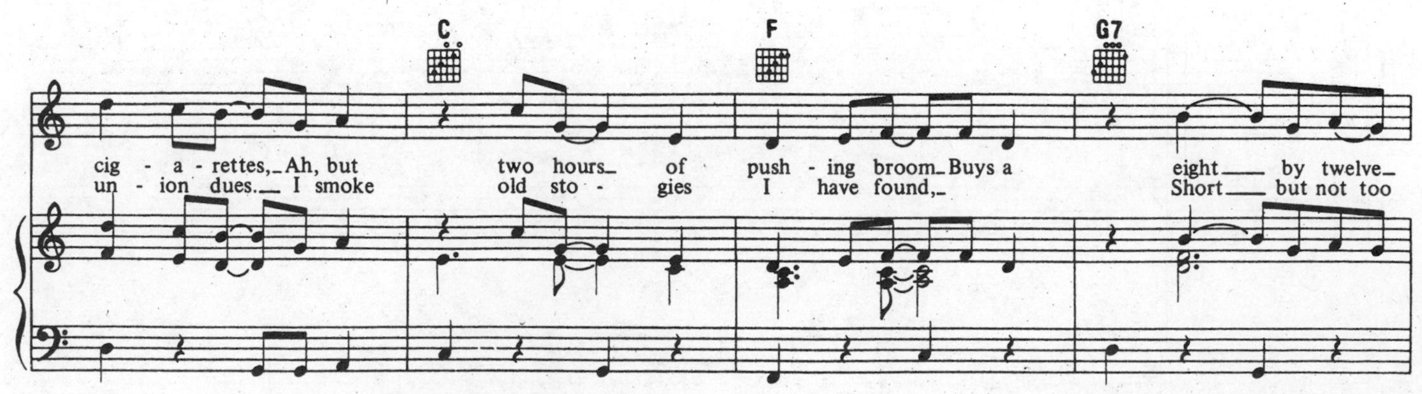

C
C7
F
G7
To Coda
four bit room.— I'm a man of means by no means, King— Of The
big a-round.—
1
C
2
C
F
Road.
Road. I know ev-er-y en-gi-neer on ev-er-y train,—
mf
G7
C
F
All of the chil-dren and all of their names— And ev-er-y hand-out in ev-er-y town,— And
G7
D.C. al Coda
ev-'ry lock that ain't locked when no one's a-round. I sing
CODA
C
Road.

LONGNECK BOTTLE

Words and Music by RICK CARNES
and STEVE WARINER

D
G
D
A7
she won't un-der - stand. Long - neck bot-tle, let go of my
D
D7
G
hand. Hey, bar - room mir-ror on
floor, seems you're un-der -
D
the wall, go stare at some - one else. Don't
neath my feet ev - 'ry - where I turn. I ought-a
E7
A7
show the world the fool I am; just keep it to your - self.
waltz right out of them swing-in' doors, but that's a step I just can't learn.

D
G7
D
Long - neck bot - tle, let go of my hand.
G7
D
Well, juke - box, don't start play-in' that song a - gain.
G7
D
'Cause there's a girl at home who loves me. You know she won't un - der - stand.
G
D
A7
To Coda
D
Long - neck bot - tle, let go of my hand.

A7
D
G7
Let go!
D
D7
G7
D
D7
G
D
G7
D

A7
D
D7
D.S. al Coda
Hey, dance_
CODA
D
hand._
D7
G7
G#dim
4fr
D/A
There's a girl_ at home_ who loves_ me. You know she won't un - der - stand._
G7
D
A7
_ Long - neck bot-tle, let go of my
D
G7
N.C.
D7
hand.
rit.

NO DOUBT ABOUT IT

Words and Music by JOHN SCOTT SHERRILL
and STEVE SESKIN

E
A
sea. And when ___ you plant a seed, it reach - es for the
blues. What good ___ is a man ___ if he has - n't got a
sea. And when ___ you plant a seed, it reach - es for the
E
B
sky. That's just ___ the way it is, no - bod - y won - ders
dream? 'Bout as good as a car ___ with no ___ gas - o - line.
sky. That's just ___ the way it is, girl, ___ with you and
E
A
why. Like cof - fee needs a cup, you know ___ that it ain't
You're the one I'm dream - in' of. Got ___ to have your
I. Like cof - fee needs a cup, you know ___ that it ain't
E
B
much good with - out ___ it. ___
love; I can't live with - out ___ it. ___
much good with - out ___ it. ___

F#m7
We were meant to be to - geth - er,
A
E
no doubt a - bout it.
F#m7
Oh, there ain't no
A
E
To Coda
doubt a - bout it.

1
2
F#m7
Like a ham - mer and a
Some - thing was
E/G#
A
E
miss - ing; it was mak - ing me blue.
But
C#m
4fr
F#7
A/B
all I ev - er need - ed was you.
B7
D.S. al Coda
Just like ev - 'ry
CODA

F#m7
A
E
No
doubt a - bout
it.
F#m7
A
Oh, there ain't no
doubt a - bout
E
F#m7
it.
There ain't no
A
E
Repeat ad lib. and Fade
doubt a - bout
it.
Oh, there ain't

LUCILLE

Words and Music by ROGER BOWLING
and HAL BYNUM

Cm
F7
B♭
sat down and asked her her name.
had a strange look on his face.
When the drinks fin - 'ly hit
The big hands were cal -
B♭7
her, she said "I'm no quit - ter but I fin - 'ly quit liv - ing on
loused, he looked like a moun - tain for a min - ute I thought I was
E♭
F7
Cm7
F
dreams, I'm hun - gry for laugh - ter and here ev - er af -
dead. But he start - ed shak - ing his big heart was break -
Cm
1
F7
B♭
- ter I'm af - ter what - ev - er the oth - er life brings."
- ing he

2
F7
Bb
In the turned to the wom-an and said: you picked a
Eb
fine time to leave me Lu - cille, with four hun - gry chil -
Bb
Eb
- dren and a crop in the field. I've had some
bad times lived through some sad times but this time your hurt - in won't

Bb
F7
Bb
heal. You picked a fine time to leave me Lu - cille.
C
Af - ter he left us I
or - dered more whis - key I thought how she made him look small.
G7
Dm
G7
From the lights of the bar - room to a rent - ed ho - tel room, we

Dm
G7
C
walked with - out talk - ing at all. She was a beau -
C7
- ty but when she came to me she must - 've thought I'd lost my mind;
F
G7
I could - n't hold her 'cause the words that he told
C
her kept com - ing back time af - ter time. You picked a

F
fine time to leave __ me Lu - cille,
with four hun - gry chil -
C
F
- dren and a crop in the field.
I've had some
C
bad times, __ lived through some sad times __ but this time your hurt - in' won't heal
G7
C
Repeat and fade
You picked a fine time to leave me Lu - cille.
You picked a

MAKE THE WORLD GO AWAY

Words and Music by
HANK COCHRAN

F
Make the world go a - way
G7
C
and get it off my shoul - ders.
F
G7
Say the things you used to say
and make the world go a -
1
C
way.
I'm sor - ry if I
2
C
way.

MAMMAS DON'T LET YOUR BABIES GROW UP TO BE COWBOYS

Words and Music by ED BRUCE
and PATSY BRUCE

G
G7
such. Mam - mas don't let your ba - bies grow
C
up to be cow - boys, 'Cause they'll
D7
nev - er stay home, and they're al - ways a - lone, E - ven with
G
D7
some - one they love.
A
A

G
G7
cow - boy ain't eas - y to love and he's hard - er to
cow - boy loves smok - y ole pool rooms and clear moun - tain
mp
C
D7
hold. And it means more to him to
morn - ings. Lit - tle warm
G
give you a song than sil - ver or gold.
pup - pies and chil - dren and girls of the night.
D7
G
G7
Bud - wei - ser buck - les and soft fad - ed
Them that don't know him won't like him and

C
Le - vis and each night be - gins a new day.
them that do some - times won't know how to take him.
D7
If you can't un - der - stand him and he don't die
He's not wrong, he's just dif - f'rent and his pride won't
G
young, He'll prob - a - bly just ride a - way.
let him do things to make you think he's right.
1 D7
2 D7
D.S. and Fade

MY BEST FRIEND

Words and Music by AIMEE MAYO
and BILL LUTHER

Moderately

N.C. A E/G# Em/G

mf

D/F# D A/C# E

A E/G# Em/G

I never had no one that I could count
You stand by me and you believe in

D/F# D A/C# E

on. I've been let down so many times.
me like nobody ever has.

A
E/G#
Em/G
And I was tired of hurt - in',
so tired of search -
When my world goes cra - zy,
you're right there to save
D/F#
D
A
- in'
till you walked in
to my life.
me.
You make me see
how much I have.
E
D
It was a feel -
And I still trem -
A
Bm7
2 fr
- in'
I'd nev - er known.
And for the first
- ble
when we touch.
And, oh, the look

A/C#
E
A
time
I did-n't feel a-lone.
in your eyes
when we make love.
You're more
E/G#
Bm7
2fr
A/C#
than a lov-er.
There could nev-er be an-
Bm7
2fr
A/C#
E
oth-er
to make me feel the way you do.
A
E/G#
Bm7
2fr
A/C#
Oh,
we just get clos-er.
I fall in love all o-

Bm7
2fr
A/C♯
Esus
E
- ver ev - 'ry time I look at you.
E/G♯
A
I don't know where I'd be with - out you here with me.
Bm7
2fr
A/C♯
D
Bm9
To Coda
Life with you makes per - fect sense. You're my best
1
A
E/G♯
Em/G
D/F♯
friend. You're my best friend,

D
A/C♯
oh, yeah.
2
E/G♯
Em/G
D/F♯
friend.
Ooh, oh, ooh, oh.
You're my best friend,
D
A/C♯
E
D.S. al Coda
uh, huh.
You're
cresc.
CODA
N.C.
A
E/G♯
Bm7
2fr
friend.
Oh, whoa, ooh, oh.

A/C
Bm7
2fr
A/C#
You're my best friend,
oh, yeah.
E
A
E/G#
Ooh,
Bm7
2fr
A/C#
Bm7
2fr
you're my best friend.
A/C#
E
Repeat and Fade
Opt. Ending
A
cresc.

NOBODY LOVES ME LIKE YOU DO

Words by PAMELA PHILLIPS
Music by JAMES P. DUNNE

B♭
C/B♭
Am7
Dm
flame to light our way, that burns bright - er ev - 'ry day;
B♭
A7
A7/C♯
Dm
F/G
G7
now I have you;
Gm7
3fr
F/A
B♭
C7
F
Am7
no - bod - y loves me like you do.
B♭
B♭/C
C7
F
C/F
Male: Like a leaf up -
Male: I was words with -
cresc.
mf

Bb
F/A
Gm7
C7
on the wind,_
out a tune._
I could find no place to
Female: I was a song still un-
Am7
Dm7
Bb
C/Bb
land.
sung.
I dreamed the hours a-way, and
Male: A po-em with no rhyme, Female: a
Am7
Dm
Bb
A7
A7/C#
Dm
F/G
G7
won-dered ev-'ry day, do dreams come true?
dan-cer out of time. Both: But now there's you.
Gm7
F/A
Bbmaj7
C7
F
C/E
F
C/E
No-bod-y loves_ me like you do.

B♭
Am7
B♭
Am7
Both: What if I nev - er met _ you?
Where would I be right now? _
f
B♭
A7
A7/C♯
Dm
G7sus
G7
Fun - ny how life just falls _ in place _ some - how. ________
Male: You
B♭
F/A
Gm7
F/A
3fr
touched my heart _ in plac - es Female: that I nev - er e - ven knew. ______
1
Gm7
F/A
B♭
C
C7sus
F
Am7
Both: No - bod - y loves _ me like you do.
dim.
mp

2
Bb
Bb/C
C7
Gm7
F/A
Bb
Both: No - bod - y loves_ me,
Gm7
F/A
Bb
no - bod - y loves_ me,
Gm7
Am7
Bbmaj7
A7/C#
no - bod - y loves_ me like you
Freely
Dm
G7sus
G7
Gm7
F/A
Bb
C
C7sus
do.
No - bod - y loves_ me like you
rit. e dim.
mp
F
Am7
Bb
Bb/C
F
do.
a tempo
rit.

OH, LONESOME ME

Words and Music by
DON GIBSON

G7
1 C
2 C
Oh, lone - some me. A me.
G
D7
I'll bet she's not like me, she's out and fan - cy free
G
Flirt - ing with the boys with all her charms But I still love her
D7
so and, broth - er, don't you know I'd wel - come her right back here in my

G
G7
C
G7
arms Well, there must be some way I can lose these lone - some blues
C
For - get a - bout the past and find some - bod - y new I've
C7
F
G7
thought of ev - 'ry - thing from A to Z oh,
C
G7
C
lone - some me.

OKIE FROM MUSKOGEE

Words and Music by MERLE HAGGARD
and ROY EDWARD BURRIS

Bb7
D. And we don't burn our draft cards down on
woo. We don't let our hair grow long and
seen. Foot-ball's still the rough-est thing on
Main Street, But we like liv-ing right and be-ing
shag-gy Like the hip-pies out in San Fran-cis-co
cam-pus, And the kids here still re-spect the Col-lege
Eb
free.
do.
Dean.
And I'm proud to be an
O-kie from Mus-ko-gee; A

Bb7
place where e - ven squares can have a ball.
We still wave Ol' Glo - ry down at the
Court House, White light - ning's still the
Eb
1,2
3
big - gest thrill of all.
3. Leath - er

ONE BOY, ONE GIRL

Words and Music by MARK ALAN SPRINGER
and SHAYE SMITH

Tenderly

C G C

mf

C/G G C G

He fin-'lly gave in ___ to his friend's _ girl - friend _ when she said, _
no time at all ___ they were stand - ing there _ in the front _

F G C

___ "There's some - one ___ you should meet." ___ At a
___ of a lit - tle ___ church, ___ a -

G F G

crowd - ed res - t'rant way ___ cross _ town _ he wait - ed im - pa - tient - ly. ___
mong their friends _ and fam - i - ly, ___ re - peat - ing those sa - cred words. _

C
Am
Dm
when she walked in, their eyes met
The preach - er said, "Son, kiss your bride,"
G
C
Am
and they both stared.
and he raised her veil.
And right there and then ev -
Like the night they met, time
Dm
G
Am
G/B
- 'ry - one else dis - ap - peared
just stood still
but
for
one boy,
C
G
Em
one girl,
two hearts beat - ing wild -

F
G
C
G
-ly. To put it mild - ly, it was love at first sight.
F
G
C
He smiled, she smiled,
G
F
C
G
and they knew right a - way
Em
Am
this was the day they'd wait - ed for all their lives.

D7sus
D
F
For a mo - ment the whole world
Dm
F
G7sus
To Coda
re - volved a - round one boy and one girl.
1 C
G
C
C/G
G
2 C
Em
In
He was hold - ing her hand when the doc -

Am
D7sus
- tor looked up and grinned.
D
F
Dm
"Con - grat - u - la - tions!
F/G
G
D.S. al Coda
CODA
C
Twins." One boy,
G
C
G
C
rit.

PLEASE REMEMBER ME

Words and Music by RODNEY CROWELL
and WILL JENNINGS

Moderately

F(add2) Am7 G/A F(add2)

mf

C C(add2) C C(add2) C

Am G F

When all our tears _ have reached the sea,

C G F

a part of you will live in me _ way down

Original key: D♭ major. This edition has been transposed down one half-step to be more playable.

C
C(add9)
C
deep in - side my heart.
C(add9)
C
Am
G
F
The days keep com - in' with - out fail.
C
G
A new wind is gon - na find your sail.
F
C
G
That's where your jour - ney starts.
You'll find

C
E7
bet - ter love, strong as it ev - er was, deep as a
3
Am
F
riv - er runs, warm as the morn - ing sun.
C
G
F
Please re - mem - ber me.
C
Am
G
Just like the waves down by the

F
C
shore,
we're gon - na keep on com - in'
G
F
back for more
'cause we don't
C
Am
G
ev - er wan - na stop.
Out in this brave new world you'll
F
C
see,
oh, the val - leys and the

G
F
peaks.
And I can see you on the
C
G
C
E7
top. You'll find bet-ter love, strong as it ev-er was,
Am
F
deep as a riv-er runs, warm as the morn-ing sun.
C
G
Please re -

To Coda
C
mem - ber me.
G
F
C
Re - mem - ber me when you're out walk - ing,
G
F
C
when snow falls high out - side your door,
G
F
C
late at night when you're not sleep - in'

F
G
and moon - light falls a - cross your floor
Am
G
F
and I can't hurt you an - y - more.
G
D.S. al Coda
You'll find
CODA
C
Em7
me.
Am
F
C/G
G
Please re -

F
Am7
G/A
mem - ber me.
F
C
Repeat and Fade
F
Am7
G/A
F
C
Optional Ending
C

RELEASE ME

Words and Music by ROBERT YOUNT,
EDDIE MILLER and DUB WILLIAMS

F C7 F Fdim B♭6/F F F7
more. To waste our lives would be a
near. Her lips are warm while yours are
me? To live a lie would bring us
B♭ F C7
sin; re - lease me and let me love a -
cold; re - lease me, my dar - ling, let me
pain, so re - lease me and let me love a -
1, 2
F C7
gain.
go.
3
F B♭ F
gain.

SHE'S EVERY WOMAN

Words and Music by VICTORIA SHAW
and GARTH BROOKS

E
E/G♯
A
B
G♯7/B♯
just like a riv - er, then she'll beg you to for - give
love on rain - y nights. She's a stroll through Christ - mas lights.
C♯m
G♯m/B
A
B7sus
her. Oh, she's ev - 'ry wom - an that I've ev - er known.
And she's ev - 'ry - thing I want to do a - gain.
E
1
2
B/D♯
C♯m
She's so New York
And
Though
it needs
A
B
C♯m
no ex - pla - na - tion,
'cause it all

A
E
makes per-fect sense.
So when it comes
B/D♯
4fr
A/C♯
E/B
F♯m
E/G♯
down to tempt - ta - tion,
she's on both sides
A
B7sus
4fr
B7
To Coda
E
E/G♯
of the fence.
A
B
G♯7/B♯
C♯m
4fr
G♯m/B
4fr
A

E/G#
B7sus
4fr
B7
Cdim
D.S. al Coda
CODA
F#m7
B7
E
E/G#
She's an - y - thing _ but typ - i - cal.
A
B
G#7/B#
C#m
4fr
G#m/B
A
She's so un - pre-dict - a - ble. _ Oh, but e - ven at _ her worst,
E/G#
B7sus
4fr
B7
she ain't _ that bad. ___ She's as real _

E
E/G♯
A
B
G♯7/B♯
as real can be and she's ev - 'ry fan - ta - sy.
C♯m
G♯m/B
A
B7sus
4fr
C♯m
Lord, she's ev - 'ry lov - er that I've ev - er had.
G♯m7
F♯m7
B7sus
E
E/G♯
And she's ev - 'ry lov - er that I've nev - er had.
A
B7sus
E
rit.

SINGING THE BLUES

Words and Music by
MELVIN ENDSLEY

Bb
F
C7
cry-ing all night 'cause ev-'ry-thing's wrong and noth-ing ain't right with-
Bb
C7
F
F7
out you. You got me sing-ing the blues. The
Bb
F
Bb
moon and stars no long-er shine, the dream is gone I
F
Bb
F
thought was mine. There's noth-ing left for me to do but

C7 F

cry ___ o - ver you ___ well, I nev - er felt more like

B♭ F C7

run - ning a - way ___ but why should I go ___ 'cause I could - n't stay ___ with -

B♭ C7 1 F B♭

out you. You got me sing - ing the blues. ___

F C7 2 F

___ Well, I blues. ___

SIXTEEN TONS

Words and Music by
MERLE TRAVIS

C7 Em Em

Chorus

mind ___ that's ___ weak ___ and a back that's strong. You load
straw - boss ___ said ___ "Well - a bless my soul." You load
high - toned ___ wo - man make me walk the line. You load
right one don't - a get you, then the left one will. You load

Six - teen Tons,

what do you get? ___ An - oth - er day old - er and deep - er in debt. ___ Saint

Am Em

Pe - ter, don't you call me 'cause I can't go ___ I owe ___ my soul to the

1,2,3 Em 4 Em

com - pa - ny store. ___

2. I was ___
3. I was
4. If you

SWEET DREAMS

Words and Music by
DON GIBSON

C F C G7 C D7 G7
you
you
You don't love me, it's plain
C D7 G7
I should know you'll nev-er wear my name
C F C Am C
I should hate you the whole night through In-stead of hav-ing
F G7
sweet dreams a-bout
1 C F C G7
you.
2 C F C
you.

TENNESSEE WALTZ

Words and Music by REDD STEWART
and PEE WEE KING

G
G7
duced him to my loved one and while they were
C
G
D7
waltz - ing my friend stole my sweet - heart from
G
B7
me. I re - mem - ber the night and the
C
G
Ten - nes - see Waltz. Now I know just how

D7
G
much I have lost.
Yes I lost my lit - tle
G7
C
dar - lin' the night they were play - ing the
G
D7
1
G
beau - ti - ful Ten - nes - see Waltz.
2
G
I was Waltz.

THREE CIGARETTES IN AN ASHTRAY

Words and Music by EDDIE MILLER
and W.S. STEVENSON

F
D7
G9
ev - ery - thing went wrong.
Now there's three cig - a - rettes
C7
Gm7
B♭/C
C7
in the ash - tray.
F
B♭(add9)
F6
F7
I watched her take him from me.
And his
B♭
F
F9
love is no long - er my own.

B♭
F
Now they are gone and I sit a-
1 D7
Gm7
C7
F
lone and watch one cig-a-rette burn a-way.
Gm7
C13
2 D7
Freely
Gm7
lone and watch one cig-a rette
C7add13
A tempo
F6
B♭6
F6/9
burn a-way.
With pedal

WALK A MILE IN MY SHOES

Words and Music by
JOE SOUTH

ADDITIONAL LYRICS

2. Now your whole world you see around you is just a reflection
And the law of karma says you reap just what you sow.
So unless you've lived a life of total perfection
You'd better be careful of every stone that you should throw.
(Chorus)

3. And yet we spend the day throwing stones at one another
'Cause I don't think or wear my hair the same way you do.
Well I may be common people but I'm your brother
And when you strike out and try to hurt me it's a-hurtin' you.
(Chorus)

4. There are people on reservations and out in the ghettos
And, brother, there but for the grace of God go you and I.
If I only had the wings of a little angel
Don't you know I'd fly to the top of the mountain and then I'd cry.
(Chorus)

WALKIN' AFTER MIDNIGHT

F C7 F B♭ F/A Gm7 F B♭7
my way__ of be-ing close to you. I go out walk-in'__ af - ter mid-night search - in' for
F B♭ F F9 Cm7 B♭ E♭7
you. I stop to see a weep-in' wil-low cry - in' on his pil-low,
F Fmaj7 F6 F7 B♭ E♭7
may - be he's cry - in' for me. And as the sky turns gloom - y night winds whis - per to me. I'm
F Adim Gm7 C7
lone - ly as lone - ly as can be. I'll go out
D.S. al Coda
CODA
F E♭7 F
me.
rit.

WALKING THE FLOOR OVER YOU

Words and Music by
ERNEST TUBB

Swingy tempo

C7
You've bro - ken your prom - ise and you
I thought that you want - ed me and
Just keep right on walk - ing and it
F7
Bb7
left me here a - lone, I don't know why you
al - ways would be mine, But you went and
won't hurt you to cry. Re - mem - ber that I
Eb
did, Dear but I do know that you're gone.
left me here with trou - bles on my mind.
love you and I will the day I die.
Chorus
Eb
I'm Walk - ing The Floor O - ver

F7
Bb7
You I can't sleep a wink, that is
Eb
C7
true I'm hop - ing and I'm pray - ing as my
F7
Bb7
heart breaks right in two, Walk - ing The Floor O - ver
1,2
Eb
F7
Bb7
3
Eb
Ab
Eb
You.
2. Now,
3. Now,
You.

WELCOME TO MY WORLD

Words and Music by RAY WINKLER
and JOHN HATHCOCK

D9
G
leave your cares be - hind,
Wel - come to my
C
D7
G
C
G
world
built with you in mind.
D7
G
D7
Knock and the door will o - pen,
Seek and you will
G
D7
G
find,
Ask and you'll be giv - en,
The

A7
D
G
key to this world of mine,
I'll be wait - ing
C
D9
G
here
with my arms un - furled
Wait - ing just for
C
D7
1 G
Am7
you,
Wel - come to my world.
D7+5
G
2 G
C
G
Wel - come to my world.
mf

WHEN MY BLUE MOON TURNS TO GOLD AGAIN

Words and Music by WILEY WALKER
and GENE SULLIVAN

Bb
Eb
Bb
F7
gold.
ry.
gold.
When my blue moon turns to gold a - gain.
When the rain - bow turns the clouds a - way;
When my
blue moon turns to gold a - gain,
You'll be back in my
arms to stay.
The
The
stay.
F6
Gm6
Eb6
1,2
3

WHEN YOU SAY NOTHING AT ALL

Words and Music by PAUL OVERSTREET
and DON SCHLITZ

Eb
Bb
Ab
Bb
3fr
4fr
what I hear when you don't say a thing.
what's be-ing said be-tween your heart and mine.
The
smile on your face lets me know that you need me. There's a truth in your eyes say-ing you'll
never leave me. A touch of your hand says you'll catch me if ev-er I fall.
Ab/C
Bb/D
Eb/G
To Coda
1
Now you say it best when you say noth-ing at all.

2
Ab
Bb
Eb
Bb/D
Ab/C
4fr
3fr
when you say noth-ing at all.
D.S. al Coda
The
CODA
rit.

WHO I AM

Words and Music by BRETT JAMES
and TROY VERGES

D
G
If I don't make ___ it to ___ the big ___
Should my ten - der heart ___ be bro -
D
C
___ leagues, if I nev - er win ___ a Gram - my, I'm
- ken, I will cry those tear - drops know - in'
Em
D
C
gon - na be ___ just fine ___ be - cause ___ I know ex - act -
I will be ___ just fine ___ be - cause ___ noth - in' chang -
G/B
Am7
D
G
- ly
- es
who ___ I ___ am. ___

D C

I am Rose - ma - ry's grand - daugh - ter, the spit - ting

D Em D/F#

im - age of my fa - ther. And when the day is done, my ma -

C D G D

- ma's still my big - gest fan. Some - times I'm clue - less and I'm clum -

C D Em

- sy, but I got friends that love me and they know

D/F♯ C D Am7

just where I stand. It's all a part

D To Coda 1 G

of me and that's who I am.

D/G C/G D 2 G

D C D Em

D/F#
C
D
I'm a
F
C
saint and I'm a sin - ner. I'm a los - er, I'm a win -
E♭
3fr
- ner. I am stead - y and un - sta - ble, I'm
D
young, but I am a - ble.

G D/G C/E D/F#

I am Rose - ma - ry's grand - daugh - ter, the spit - ting im - age of my

Em D/F# C D

fa - ther. And when the day is done, my ma - ma's still my big - gest fan.

G D

Some - times I'm clue - less and I'm clum -

C D Em

- sy, but I got friends that love me and they know

D/F#
C
D
Am7
where I stand.
It's all a part
D
D.S. al Coda
of me
and that's who I am.
CODA
G
D
C
D
Em
That's who I am.
D
C
Am7
G

WHY ME?
(Why Me, Lord?)

Words and Music by
KRIS KRISTOFFERSON

C G D7

Lord, help me, Je - sus, I've wast - ed it so, Help me, Je - sus, I know what I

G G7 C G

am. ____ But now that I know that I've need - ed you So, help me

D7 To Coda 1 G D7 2 G G7 D.S. al Coda

Je - sus, my soul's in your hands. Try me, Lord hands.

CODA G D7 C Bm Am G

hands. ____ Je - sus, my soul's in your hands. ____

slower

WRITE THIS DOWN

Words and Music by KENT ROBBINS
and DANA HUNT

B♭7
E♭
3fr
blind.
Thought ev - 'ry - thing was go - in' all right,
'Cause ev - 'ry sin - gle word is true
A♭
4fr
E♭
3fr
but I was run - nin' out of time.
and I think you need to know.
'Cause you had one
So use it as a
A♭
4fr
B♭7
foot out the door.
book - mark,
I swear I did - n't see.
stick it on your 'fridg - er - a - tor door,
D♭
E♭
3fr
But if you're real - ly go - in' a - way,
here's some fin - al words from me.
hang it in a pic - ture frame up a - bove the man - tle where you'll see it for

Ab
Db
Ab
Eb
4fr
3fr
sure.
Ba - by, write this
Ab
Bb7
down, take a lit - tle note to re - mind you in case you did - n't
Db
know. Tell your - self I love you and I don't want you to
Eb
Ab
Eb
go. Write this down. Take my

A♭
4fr
words and read 'em ev - 'ry day. Keep 'em close
B♭9
by, don't you let 'em fade a - way. So you'll re -
D♭
E♭
3fr
To Coda
1
A♭
4fr
mem-ber what I for - got to say, write this down.
B♭9

Eb7
Ab
Eb7
I'll sign it at the
2
Ab
down.
Cm7
You can find a
chis - el,
Eb
I can find a

D♭
stone.
Folks 'll be read - in' these words
E♭
3fr
E♭/D♭
3fr
Cm
3fr
E♭/B♭
6fr
D.S. al Coda
long af - ter we're gone. Ba - by, write this
CODA
A♭
4fr
B♭9
down.
Oh, I love you and I don't want you to
E♭
3fr
A♭
4fr
D♭
A♭
4fr
go.
Ba - by, write this down.

YOU ARE MY SUNSHINE

Words and Music by JIMMIE DAVIS
and CHARLES MITCHELL

F7
B♭
When I a - woke, dear, I was mis -
But if you leave me to love an -
But now you've left me and love an -
F
C7
tak - en and I hung my
oth - er, you'll re - gret it
oth - er; You have shat - tered
F
head and cried:
all som - day.
all my dreams.
You are my
Fdim
F
sun - shine, my on - ly sun - shine,

F7
Bb
— you make me hap - py when skies are
F
F7
Bb
gray. You'll nev - er know, dear, how much I
F
C7
love you; Please don't take my sun - shine a -
1,2
F
3
F
F6/9
Fmaj7
way. { I'll al - ways / You told me } way.
rit.

YOUR CHEATIN' HEART

Words and Music by
HANK WILLIAMS

C7
F
Ab7
the whole night through Your Cheat - in'
when you'll be blue Your Cheat - in'
mf
mp
mf
G7
C
Heart will tell on you
Heart will tell on you
mp
C7
F
When tears come down like fall - in'
When tears come down like fall - in'
mf
C
D7
rain You'll toss a - round
rain You'll toss a - round

G7
and call my name
and call my name
You'll walk the
You'll walk the
C
C7
F
floor
floor
the way I do
the way I do
mp
mf
mp
Ab7
G7
Your Cheat - in' Heart
Your Cheat - in' Heart
will tell on
will tell on
mf
1
C
G7
2
C
you.
Your Cheat - in'
you.
mp
mf
mp
rit.
mf

YOU CAN'T MAKE A HEART LOVE SOMEBODY

Words and Music by STEVE CLARK
and JOHNNY MacRAE

G
pock - et, ___ think-in' now's the per-fect time.
know of ___ to make the feel-ing grow.
G7
When he popped the ques - tion, he could see the tear - drops fill her
I've begged and I've plead - ed with my heart, but there's _ no get-tin'
C
D
eyes. She said, "I knew this was com - in' and I'm
through. My heart's the on - ly part ___ of
G
sor - ry, ___ but I hope you re - al - ize."
me _______ that's not in love _ with _ you."

D/F#
Em
G7/D
You can't make a heart love some - bod - y. You can
C
G
D
C
tell it what to do, but it won't lis - ten at all.
G
D/F#
Em
D
You can't make a heart love some - bod - y. You can
C
G
1 D
To Coda
lead a heart to love, but you can't make it fall.

G
D/F#
C
Then she
2
D
G
can't make it fall.
D.S. al Coda
CODA
D
G
can't make it fall.
You can
C
G
lead a heart to love,
but you
D
G
D
G
can't make it fall.
rit.

YOU HAD ME FROM HELLO

Words and Music by SKIP EWING
and KENNY CHESNEY

D
A/C#
just cap-tured me. And
Bm
A/B
G
you were in my fu - ture, far as I could see. And I
A
G
D
don't know how it hap - pened, but it hap-pened still. You ask
Bm
A/B
G
A7sus
A
me if I love you, if I al - ways will. Well,

D
A/D
G
A
you had me from hel - lo. I felt love start to grow
D/F#
Bm7
2fr
G
the mo - ment that I looked in - to your eyes,
D/A
A
D
A/D
G
you owned me. It was o - ver from the start. You com-plete -
A
D
Bm7
2fr
- ly stole my heart and now you won't let go.

G
Em7
I nev - er e - ven had
a chance, you know.
A7sus
To Coda
A7
You had me from hel - lo.
D
A/D
G
D
A/D
G
G/A
In - side

D
A/C#
I built a wall so
Bm
A/B
G
high a - round my heart I thought I'd nev-er fall.
3
G/A
D
A/C#
One touch, you brought it down,
Bm
A/B
G
the bricks of my de-fens - es scat-tered on the ground.

A
G
And I swore to me I was - n't gon - na love
D
Bm
A/B
a - gain. The last time was the last time I
D.S. al Coda
G
A7sus
A/C#
let some - one in. But
CODA
A7
D
me from hel - lo.
A/C#
3
Bm
That's all you said. Some - thin' in your voice

A/B
G
A7sus
D
caused me to turn my head. You had me from hel - lo.
A/D
G
A/C#
D
You had me from hel - lo.
A/D
G
A7
D
Girl, I've loved you from hel - lo.
A/D
G
A7sus
A7
D
rit.

THE BEST EVER COLLECTION

ARRANGED FOR PIANO, VOICE AND GUITAR

100 of the Most Beautiful Piano Solos Ever
100 songs
00102787 .... $27.50

150 of the Most Beautiful Songs Ever
150 ballads
00360735 .... $27.00

150 More of the Most Beautiful Songs Ever
150 songs
00311318 .... $29.99

More of the Best Acoustic Rock Songs Ever
69 tunes
00311738 .... $19.95

Best Acoustic Rock Songs Ever
65 acoustic hits
00310984 .... $19.95

Best Big Band Songs Ever
68 big band hits
00359129 .... $17.99

Best Blues Songs Ever
73 blues tunes
00312874 .... $19.99

Best Broadway Songs Ever
83 songs
00309155 .... $24.99

More of the Best Broadway Songs Ever
82 songs
00311501 .... $22.95

Best Children's Songs Ever
102 songs
00310358 .... $19.99

Best Christmas Songs Ever
69 holiday favorites
00359130 .... $24.99

Best Classic Rock Songs Ever
64 hits
00310800 .... $22.99

Best Classical Music Ever
86 classical favorites
00310674 (Piano Solo) $19.95

The Best Country Rock Songs Ever
52 hits
00118881 .... $19.99

Best Country Songs Ever
78 classic country hits
00359135 .... $19.99

Best Disco Songs Ever
50 songs
00312565 .... $19.99

Best Dixieland Songs Ever
90 songs
00312326 .... $19.99

Best Early Rock 'n' Roll Songs Ever
74 songs
00310816 .... $19.95

Best Easy Listening Songs Ever
75 mellow favorites
00359193 .... $19.95

Best Gospel Songs Ever
80 gospel songs
00310503 .... $19.99

Best Hymns Ever
118 hymns
00310774 .... $18.99

Best Jazz Piano Solos Ever
80 songs
00312079 .... $19.99

Best Jazz Standards Ever
77 jazz hits
00311641 .... $19.95

More of the Best Jazz Standards Ever
74 beloved jazz hits
00311023 .... $19.95

Best Latin Songs Ever
67 songs
00310355 .... $19.99

Best Love Songs Ever
65 favorite love songs
00359198 .... $19.95

Best Movie Songs Ever
71 songs
00310063 .... $19.99

Best Praise & Worship Songs Ever
80 all-time favorites
00311057 .... $22.99

More of the Best Praise & Worship Songs Ever
76 songs
00311800 .... $24.99

Best R&B Songs Ever
66 songs
00310184 .... $19.95

Best Rock Songs Ever
63 songs
00490424 .... $18.95

Best Showtunes Ever
71 songs
00118782 .... $19.99

Best Songs Ever
72 must-own classics
00359224 .... $24.99

Best Soul Songs Ever
70 hits
00311427 .... $19.95

Best Standards Ever, Vol. 1 (A-L)
72 beautiful ballads
00359231 .... $17.95

Best Standards Ever, Vol. 2 (M-Z)
73 songs
00359232 .... $17.99

More of the Best Standards Ever, Vol. 1 (A-L)
76 all-time favorites
00310813 .... $17.95

More of the Best Standards Ever, Vol. 2 (M-Z)
75 stunning standards
00310814 .... $17.95

Best Torch Songs Ever
70 sad and sultry favorites
00311027 .... $19.95

Best Wedding Songs Ever
70 songs
00311096 .... $19.95

Prices, contents and availability subject to change without notice. Not all products available outside the U.S.A.

HAL•LEONARD® CORPORATION
7777 W. BLUEMOUND RD. P.O. BOX 13819 MILWAUKEE, WI 53213

Visit us online for complete songlists at www.halleonard.com

0714

Get more BANG for your buck! with budgetbooks

These value-priced collections feature over 300 pages of piano/vocal/guitar arrangements. With at least 70 hit songs in most books, you pay 18 cents or less for each song!

Prices, contents & availability subject to change without notice.

HAL•LEONARD®
CORPORATION
7777 W. BLUEMOUND RD. P.O. BOX 13819
MILWAUKEE, WISCONSIN 53213

www.halleonard.com

ACOUSTIC
66 unplugged jewels: American Pie • Blackbird • Leaving on a Jet Plane • More Than Words • Scarborough Fair • Tears in Heaven • Time in a Bottle • Wonderwall • more.
00311857 P/V/G $12.99

ACOUSTIC HITS
Make the most out of your money with this collection of 58 hits: Bridge over Troubled Water • Falling Slowly • Hallelujah • Love Story • The Night They Drove Old Dixie Down • Wish You Were Here • and more.
00103681 P/V/G $12.99

BLUES SONGS
99 blues classics packed into one affordable collection! Includes: All Your Love • Born Under a Bad Sign • Killing Floor • Pride and Joy • Sweet Home Chicago • The Thrill Is Gone • more!
00311499 P/V/G $12.95

BROADWAY SONGS
This jam-packed collection features 73 songs from 56 shows, including: Any Dream Will Do • Cabaret • Getting to Know You • I Dreamed a Dream • One • People • You'll Never Walk Alone • and more.
00310832 P/V/G $12.99

CHILDREN'S SONGS
This fabulous collection includes over 100 songs that kids love, including: Alphabet Song • London Bridge • On Top of Spaghetti • Sesame Street Theme • You've Got a Friend in Me • and more.
00311054 P/V/G $12.99

CHRISTMAS SONGS
100 holiday favorites, includes: All I Want for Christmas Is You • Away in a Manger • Feliz Navidad • The First Noel • Merry Christmas, Darling • O Holy Night • Silver Bells • What Child Is This? • and more.
00310887 P/V/G $12.99

CLASSIC ROCK
A priceless collection of 70 of rock's best at a price that can't be beat! Includes: Ballroom Blitz • Bohemian Rhapsody • Gloria • Pink Houses • Rhiannon • Roxanne • Summer of '69 • Wild Thing • You Really Got Me • and more.
00310906 P/V/G $12.99

CONTEMPORARY CHRISTIAN
52 CCM faves in a value-priced songbook: All to You • Be Near • Breathe • Deeper • I Wanna Sing • King • Maker of All Things • Oceans from the Rain • Pray • Song of Love • These Hands • Wisdom • more.
00311732 P/V/G $12.95

CONTEMPORARY HITS
A cost-saving collection of 53 favorites, including: Amazed • Angel • Breathe • Clocks • Don't Know Why • Drops of Jupiter (Tell Me) • A Moment Like This • Smooth • Superman (It's Not Easy) • Underneath It All • and more.
00311053 P/V/G $12.99

COUNTRY SONGS
A great collection of 90 songs, including: Always on My Mind • Amazed • Boot Scootin' Boogie • Down at the Twist and Shout • Friends in Low Places • Okie from Muskogee • Sixteen Tons • Walkin' After Midnight • You Are My Sunshine • and more.
00310833 P/V/G $12.99

EARLY ROCK
You can't go wrong with this collection of over 90 early rock classics, including: All Shook Up • Blue Suede Shoes • Bye Bye Love • Fun, Fun, Fun • Hello Mary Lou • Hound Dog • In My Room • Louie, Louie • Peggy Sue • Shout • Splish Splash • Tequila • and more.
00311055 P/V/G $12.95

FOLK SONGS
148 of your all-time folk favorites! Includes: Camptown Races • Danny Boy • Greensleeves • Home on the Range • Shenandoah • Skip to My Lou • Yankee Doodle • and many more.
00311841 P/V/G $12.99

GOSPEL SONGS
Over 100 songs, including: Behold the Lamb • Down by the Riverside • Daddy Sang Bass • In Times like These • Midnight Cry • We Are So Blessed • The Wonder of It All • and many more.
00311734 P/V/G $12.99

HYMNS
150 beloved hymns in a money-saving collection: Amazing Grace • Come, Thou Fount of Every Blessing • For the Beauty of the Earth • Holy, Holy, Holy • O Worship the King • What a Friend We Have in Jesus • many more!
00311587 P/V/G $12.99

JAZZ STANDARDS
A collection of over 80 jazz classics. Includes: Alfie • Bewitched • Blue Skies • Body and Soul • Fever • I'll Be Seeing You • In the Mood • Isn't It Romantic? • Mona Lisa • Stella by Starlight • When Sunny Gets Blue • and more.
00310830 P/V/G $12.99

LATIN SONGS
An invaluable collection of over 80 Latin standards. Includes: Desafinado (Off Key) • Frenesí • How Insensitive (Insensatez) • La Bamba • Perfidia • Spanish Eyes • So Nice (Summer Samba) • and more.
00311056 P/V/G $12.99

LOVE SONGS
This collection of over 70 favorite love songs includes: And I Love Her • Crazy • Endless Love • Longer • (You Make Me Feel Like) A Natural Woman • You Are So Beautiful • You Are the Sunshine of My Life • and more.
00310834 P/V/G $12.99

MOVIE SONGS
Over 70 memorable movie moments, including: Almost Paradise • Cole's Song • Funny Girl • Puttin' On the Ritz • She • Southampton • Take My Breath Away (Love Theme) • Up Where We Belong • The Way We Were • and more.
00310831 P/V/G $12.99

POP/ROCK
This great collection of 75 top pop hits features: Barbara Ann • Crimson and Clover • Dust in the Wind • Hero • Jack and Diane • Lady Marmalade • Stand by Me • Tequila • We Got the Beat • What's Going On • and more.
00310835 P/V/G $12.99

SHOWTUNES
80 songs, including: And All That Jazz • Camelot • Easter Parade • Hey, Look Me Over • I Remember It Well • If I Were a Rich Man • Try to Remember • Why Can't You Behave? • Wouldn't It Be Loverly • and more.
00311849 P/V/G $12.99

STANDARDS
Nearly 80 standards, including: Boogie Woogie Bugle Boy • Don't Get Around Much Anymore • In the Still of the Night • Misty • Pennies from Heaven • So in Love • What a Diff'rence a Day Made • Witchcraft • and more.
00311853 P/V/G $12.99